Secret of the Stairs

*Your Quest for Intimacy
with Abba Father*

Ron Phillips

world
PUBLISHING
SINCE 1928

Printed in the United States of America
1 2 3 4 5 — 09 08 07 06 05

*I dedicate this book to
the leadership team and members
of Abba's House. You have my
profound gratitude for allowing me time to spend
discovering the secret place
of the Most High.*

Contents

Acknowledgments

I want to thank Randy Elliott for his encouragement in completion of this book. I appreciate Ramona Richards and all the team at World Publishing for their timely support.

Here at Abba's House, I am especially thankful to Margy Barber for her excellent assistance with the manuscript.

In addition, my heartfelt thanks to Ken Hartley, the worship team, and Abba's Army choir and orchestra for turning the "stairs" into an escalator!

Finally, let me thank Rusty Guenther for his leadership of our students who are learning to "dwell in the secret place of the Most High."

There is a place of quiet rest,
Near to the heart of God.
A place where sin cannot molest,
Near to the heart of God.

There is a place of comfort sweet,
Near to the heart of God.
A place where we our Savior meet,
Near to the heart of God.

There is a place of full release,
Near to the heart of God.
A place where all is joy and peace,
Near to the heart of God.

O Jesus, blest Redeemer,
Sent from the heart of God,
Hold us who wait before Thee
Near to the heart of God.

—Cleland B. McAfee

THE UPWARD CALL

Introduction

He stood calmly, alone and quiet in the middle of the park, the gloom of the overcast day casting a gray shadow across his young face as he gazed steadily into the sky. His hand firmly gripped a thin line of worn string.

The little boy had not gone unnoticed; many passersby looked wistfully at the scene, wishing they could pause in their hurried day and join the lad. But the only one who made time to stop was the tough neighborhood bully. Wandering by, he caught sight of the lone child, and tauntingly called out, "Hey, what'cha doin' out there, Billy?"

Billy smiled and replied, "Flying my kite!"

Scanning the cloudy sky, the bully scoffed, "I don't see a thing! Bet your kite is long gone! Bet it's not even up there!"

The lad just turned back to his string with another smile. "Oh, it is there, all right. You see, I can feel the tug . . ."

I know I can feel that pull upward, can't you? It is a call from above that beckons us to something beyond ourselves! The human soul and spirit have an innate desire to soar beyond our natural world. I believe that it is possible to have your feet on the clay of the earth while your soul flies into the heavenlies!

Do you long to follow the call?

Where is that place of quiet release and peace?

How do you get there?

When life is at its most suffocating, and you find yourself wondering how you can take even one more step through the decisions, turmoil, and stress that the journey brings—you can know a place of sweet escape and boundless peace.

You can know the secret of the stairs!

Chapter 1

The Secret
of the Stairs

What does a person do when he's at the end of his rope?

Centuries ago, there lived a young German monk. This devoted man took his holy orders seriously. His life was one of discipline. He had surrendered everything and viewed soberly the holy obligation of the church. Still, his struggling heart was empty. His love and passion could not find his Beloved.

Finally, the young cleric decided that pilgrimage and penance was the way to God. He crawled up the high stairs in Rome where many made their pilgrimages, the staircase known as Scala Santa. Worn out and bloody from the journey, there was still no answer from God.

Returning home, he was browsing in a library when he came across a complete copy of the Latin scriptures. He was astounded, for he had never held the entire word of God in his hands, in spite of years of Bible study as a monk! That day, the light came powerfully to Martin Luther as one verse from God's Word broke over his soul—"The just shall live by faith" (Ro 1:17).

Luther knew that Paul had written those words, echoing the prophet Habakkuk, to the church at Rome. Now, 1,500 years later, the same truth that had become almost smothered by church traditions and lost burst again on the stage of history to bring rebirth.

In that moment of revelation, Martin Luther had a profound conversion and filling of the Holy Spirit. He moved from religious ritual to personal relationship with Jesus. He had taken the wrong stairs at first. Now at last, he made the journey to Jesus and to freedom and went on to lead thousands of others to that same freedom!

Discovering an Empty Heart

Not unlike Luther, in 1989 I came to realize my own life had become one of religious works done to please God and to rise in denominational prestige and position. My early passion had been swallowed by religious obligation. I boasted a Puritan work ethic, so I worked hard and achieved a modicum of success, if nickels and noses were any measure in church life. After twenty-two years in the ministry, I found myself empty and powerless.

My walls were lined with books I had mastered, a few I had written, degrees I had earned, and awards I'd received. Yet, I had no close relationship with God. I had received His salvation, had dedicated my life to ministry, yet my soul was emaciated, starved for spiritual things.

My pride in my knowledge kept me from talking about my hunger. I was opinionated and mean-spirited to those who didn't agree with me. Being right was more important to me than being righteous. God graciously began to allow disappointment and difficulty to exhaust my flesh. I became so miserable that I could no longer stand myself, nor did I feel I could continue as a pastor. My life had reached critical mass. Something had to give.

Then, my life was overturned completely by what some call the baptism of the Holy Spirit. Up until that heavenly invasion, I had my faith neatly stacked into an orderly package. I believed that God did great things in the past and one day in heaven I would see Him. I was thoroughly orthodox, and adamantly opposed the "mystics" who believed God could speak, act, and touch people like He did in the book of Acts. Like a Pharisee, I had turned the written Word into an idol. I was a "Scripture expert" but a miserable failure at life.

Oh, blessed invasion! Oh, divine disruption! God met me in a hotel room in New Mexico! I had a literal and personal awakening in the long night of my despair. God spoke to me, baptized me, filled me, and called me to an authentic relationship with Him. From that new relationship would flow a new ministry, wild and free like a rushing river.

This experience was not an end but the beginning of a fantastic journey into an intimacy with Jesus. For over a decade, I have been in hot pursuit of God. This passionate quest has led me beyond the baptism of the Spirit to a desire to dwell in His presence.

Walking Where He Walked

How precious are those moments in time when eternity breaks through! So it was for me when I led three dozen travelers in Jerusalem. I was shepherding the group around the old city of Jerusalem, and the next stop was to be "the upper room" where Jesus and His disciples shared the Passover meal. I was already emotionally charged, having walked the Via Dolorosa, the way of the cross, and also toured "the pavement" under Saint Anne's Church where scholars believe our Lord Jesus walked, endured trial, and shed drops of blood from His beating.

As we journeyed, a video crew from Israeli television was trailing us. The reporter was a young Israeli woman. She asked for an interview, which I granted. She got right to the point, asking, "Why are you here in Israel?" All of a sudden I felt a rush of wind in my face and "the Presence" of Jesus flooded over me! This is what came out of my mouth: "I am in love with a Jew and wanted to see His country."

Her shocked look changed to a warm smile when I added, "By the way, His name is Jesus of Nazareth. He lived here and rose again in this wonderful land. I am head over heels, passionately in love with Him. Furthermore, on my worst day He loved me fervently."

To my amazement that evening, there I was all over Israel on the evening news declaring my love and passion for Jesus!

Late that evening, I sat alone on the balcony of my room at the Crown Plaza. I was high up in the hotel, and the panorama of Jerusalem's lights was breathtaking. It was near the end of Hanukkah, the festival of lights, and the city was glowing with candlelight in every window. From my window, the stars exploded in glory over my head. I could see across the border into Jordan, ancient Moab! The city of Amman glowed in the distance. I began to sob as I thought of the footfalls that had echoed across the ancient hills of this "capital city of the universe."

I could picture Abraham trudging up Mt. Moriah, preparing to sacrifice his only son, Isaac. I thought of Moses, looking toward Jerusalem from Mt. Nebo yet not permitted to come. I could hear again the shouts of Joshua as the Jordan River parted and the children of Israel crossed over to the Promised Land. The voices of the prophets now silent had left a permanent echo on the written record of Scripture. Amos, with his fiery threats; Hosea's love for a wayward wife; Isaiah's prophetic vision; and Jeremiah's tears all happened in this place.

I sobbed as I fell to my knees! Here is where He came, and here is where He walked, worshipped, and wept. Here that timeless trail of blood was shed for my sins.

The theological became personal, and I sobbed out my love for Jesus.

Why should those moments of passion be rare or fleeting? How sad that over time, Jesus too often becomes only a subject to study, a religious code word, or simply an icon! But He lived, and lives! The glorious Christ who came down summoned me up to the stars that evening in Israel, and the love I had for Him overflowed. Like Jacob I saw the angelic escalator, the stairs that ran both up and down! I felt as if I was caught away—I could not move but I was moving. I was empty and full! I was hungry and satisfied. I was alone and companioned by angels!

I felt that experience could be like what Paul talked about when He spoke of "the heavenlies." It was a moment when the eternal dimension intersects with time and interrupts our schedule to manifest the love that is more lasting.

Finding a Forever Friend

Too many have stopped at the moment of their Holy Spirit filling to "play" with the gifts they received, like a child on Christmas morning. Unfortunately, that is not what God intends when He places such an intimate moment of power upon us. Scripture calls the baptism of the Spirit "an earnest" or down payment of what is to come. God fills us to empower us to go on with our lives into an intimate, daily walk with Him.

Do we really believe that God allowed His Beloved Son to be savagely beaten, mocked, and crucified so we could argue about doctrine, about church policies, or about theological differences? Did God permit His Son to shed His blood in the horrors of Calvary only so we could chatter in tongues to each other? Is it feasible that the terrors of the cross fell upon our Savior simply so we could argue our denominational distinctives? And most critical—did Jesus die so that we could cower in smug isolation, while the world outside our walls flounders in desperation, looking for a true, never-ending love?

No! Jesus died so that all who believe could have a forever friendship with Him. He sent His Holy Spirit so that relationship could begin now. He wants us to be "spiritual insiders."

It was during my own pursuit that I began to discover the secret of the stairs.

Chapter 2

Runaway Bride

Imagine the parents who receive a phone call from their son or daughter, announcing suddenly, "Well, mom, dad—we got married!" The eagerness and passion of youth called to them, and in love, they ran away to tie the knot!

In Song of Solomon, we read of a lover who comes for his bride, imploring her to run away with him! This beautiful book is actually a song. To those who are old-fashioned and prudish, the Song of Solomon may seem embarrassing, intimate, and passionate! But within this tender song, we find a special word to those of us hungry for intimacy with God, a summons upward to a deeper walk with the Savior, a call to a glorious "*there*"!

The song unfolds with the story of a young girl who falls in love with a shepherd who is King Solomon, incognito. Her love is not based on the outward, but the inward. She falls in love with a shepherd and finds out when he comes for her that he is actually a king!

The book of Song of Solomon depicts the intimacy of husband and wife, and typifies Christ's love for His people. Our Lord and Lover came to us first as the Shepherd. "I am the good shepherd. The good shepherd lays down his life for the sheep" (Jo 10:11 NIV).

We fell in love with Him as a good Shepherd who was willing to lead us, feed us, love us, and die for us. It is a most amazing picture, and hard to comprehend, that the King of the Universe loves us and desires fellowship with us.

God inspired the theme of this book at a time that I was reading devotionally in the Song of Solomon. As I read, the Holy Spirit began to make the words become alive and personal to me. I felt as if I was being invited to go away with my Lord and my great Lover to a private rendezvous. I could sense the ardent passion of Jesus for me! The words jumped off the page:

My beloved spake, and said unto me, Rise up, my love, my fair one,
and come away.

For, lo, the winter is past, the rain is over and gone;

The flowers appear on the earth; the time of the singing of birds is
come, and the voice of the turtle is heard in our land;

The fig tree putteth forth her green figs, and the vines with the
tender grape give a good smell. Arise, my love, my fair one,
and come away.

O my dove, that art in the clefts of the rock, in *the secret places of the
stairs*, let me see thy countenance, let me hear thy voice; for
sweet is thy voice, and thy countenance is comely.

Song of Solomon 2:10-14 KJV, emphasis added

What is it that first summons me away from my regular duties? It is His
powerful Word! Not simply ink on a page, it is a voice sounding out His
desire off that page. I can hear the flow of His sweet Voice luring me away
from the ordinary. I think of the beautiful old song:

I come to the garden alone
While the dew is still on the roses
And the Voice I hear falling on my ear
The Son of God discloses. . . .

–Charles Miles

The Leaping Lover

Walking through the passages of the Song of Solomon is like taking a
journey into a lover's private rendezvous. God's interest in us is intense
and personal. Look with eyes of faith, and you'll see Him who is One who
comes "leaping upon the mountains, skipping over the hills" (Song 2:8).
He is our Bridegroom, and He is excited about spending time with His
beloved bride! He longs to spend time with us!

Think of those mountains as the challenges that loom before us, those
things that seem impossible to surmount but are under His feet. All the
towering difficulties that have cast their shadow over our journey are
nothing to the One we love. Are you facing something troubling? Look

ahead, for He is coming—showing up in your life just when the journey seems too difficult. The mountains are nothing to Him! He comes leaping, gladly flying to our aid.

Sometimes as He draws near, new obstacles and walls leap up to block His way. So often our Lord cannot get to us because of the walls we have erected ourselves. These are walls of sin, preoccupation, fear, and pride. Still, His love drives Him on until He finds a window and a lattice to peer through. "My beloved is like a gazelle or a young stag. Behold, he stands behind our wall; He is looking through the windows, Gazing through the lattice" (Song 2:9). His love for us drives Him onward until we notice His gaze.

His voice calls across all barriers and boundaries. "Rise up, my love, my fair one, And come away" (Song 2:10).

The Sweet Escape with the Bride

You see, we have a choice to make. We can stay put in our complacency, or take the risk and run away with Jesus. The words *rise up* mean to step up with excitement. We are called not to a dull, boring life, but to an amazing journey with our Lord.

When you are in the secret place, any doubts you have about the journey flee. His sweet voice soon removes all questions.

> The flowers appear on the earth;
> The time of singing has come,
> And the voice of the turtledove
> Is heard in our land. The fig tree puts forth her green figs,
> And the vines with the tender grapes
> Give a good smell.
> Rise up, my love, my fair one,
> And come away.
>
> Song of Solomon 2:12-13

The long, cold, lonely winter can be over in that secret place with God! The days of coldness, darkness, and death are ended. Spring heralds new life, new beginnings, and the resurrection of all nature.

The picture painted of our meeting with Him is poignant. Flowers cover the hills and valleys in a lavish display of God's greatness. The fruits of the earth are ripening to give away their sweetness. All of nature sings to His glory. The time for mourning is over and the time for music has come.

How much this is like our Lord who came over the hill of Calvary, knocked down every wall, and called us to His side. The long winter of human despair ended the day He got up from the grave. He is alive and in love! Passionately, He summons His bride again, "Rise up and come away."

Lured by both His sweet presence and His sure promise of renewal, we take the risk and go after Him. In His strong arms, we dance and leap upon the hills. Finally, coming to a distant mountain, we see stairs leading upward into a shining cloud.

"O my dove, that art in the clefts of the rock, in the secret places of the stairs, let me see thy countenance, let me hear thy voice; for sweet is thy voice, and thy countenance is comely" (Song 2:14 KJV).

He is taking us to His secret place where He has promised to show us the *secret of the stairs*. Stairs are for getting to a higher place. Stairs are for climbing. Stairs give access. But the best part is, we do not have to climb—we ascend in His arms!

But now that we stand at the foot of the stairs, what happens next? I look upward and know without a doubt that He is there to meet me personally. Gently in His grip, I gratefully take a step upward. The stairs are leading to something not yet revealed; a sovereign secret is about to be shown me. We make our way upward into the haze that I suddenly feel is part of the aura of His presence. God has brought me into His glory! The weight of it, His kabod, weighs me down. He lifts me gently and carries me onward. We come to a cleft in the Rock, and we go into a brilliantly glowing room. What is the secret I am about to behold?

I see before me, more brilliant than I could ever imagine, the Lord Jesus Christ. He shines forth with light of divine glory. I cannot help myself; I cry out to Him, "let me see your face" (Song 2:14).

Soon, I behold Him, His tender countenance still marked with the scars of thorns and savage treatment. I cry out again, "let me hear your voice" (Song 2:14).

Music fills the room, and He begins to sing His love song over me. My heart and voice shout together, "your voice is sweet, And your face is lovely" (Song 2:14).

Suddenly, I know the secret of the stairs! I can have face-to-face, voice-to-ear, and heart-to-heart communion with Jesus *now*! I don't have to wait until the "sweet by and by"! He is here when I need Him most, in the "difficult now and now"!

In truth, the church has been expecting Jesus to come for her. He will return one day. But right now, Jesus ministers to His bride to draw her away, strengthen her, and love her until she is a glorious church standing pure and powerful. There is a stairway upward available to all who are ready to run away into His arms.

The Bridegroom Calls

Again I think of Song of Solomon 2:14: "O my dove, that art in the clefts of the rock, in the secret places of the stairs, let me see thy countenance, let me hear thy voice; for sweet is thy voice, and thy countenance is comely" (KJV).

In beautiful language, the bridegroom invites his bride to come away to a private place where she will enjoy the secret of the stairs. The bridegroom is a clear symbol of Jesus and the bride represents all of us in the church. The Lord chose the imagery of husband and wife to describe what He desires. God's great heart seeks after lost, hurting souls—not so we can see how large our church rolls can become, but that they might come to worship Him!

Can you hear the call from the heights of the stairs? It is a gracious invitation to make the climb to a secret place, to embrace a special relationship with Jesus. The Lord is not simply seeking people. He is seeking worshippers. He is seeking those who will drink of His eternal fountains and find satisfaction and joy in Him. The Lover of your soul promises, "Whoever drinks of the water that I shall give him will never thirst. But the water that I shall give him will become in him a fountain of water springing up into everlasting life" (Jo 4:13-14). Will you seek Him in the secret place?

Chapter 3

Where Is "There"?

Through the ages, men and women have found themselves floundering, in over their heads in the course of life! How natural to long for a haven—somewhere safe where the trouble and turbulence cannot touch you!

The prophet Elijah knew what it was to wish for a safe escape! He had obeyed God and stood up to the treacherous King Ahab, delivering the unpopular news that a severe famine was to hit the land. Elijah no doubt feared for his life after speaking such a dramatic, prophetic word, but God made provision for him. First Kings 17:3-4 states: "Get away from here and turn eastward, and hide by the Brook Cherith, which flows into the Jordan. And it will be that you shall drink from the brook, and I have commanded the ravens to feed you there."

Since Eden, all sons and daughters of Adam have been trying to get back *there*, trying to discover *there*. They hope for a better life, a greater reality, deeper meaning, or more purpose in life. The children of Israel journeyed across a wilderness for 40 years looking for *there*. Abraham left a suburban home in the city of Ur to live in a tent because he was looking for *there*. David looked also, on the side of the hill with sheep, talking about green pastures and still waters. He was looking for *there*.

Did you know you can find *there*? *There* is not a geographical location, not a place you can find on a map. *There* is none other than the supernatural presence of God breaking through into the planet earth and releasing His supernatural provision—into YOUR life!

There Is not *Here*!

All through this book, we will address the question of how you can get *there*—to that place of intimate fellowship with God. Before anything else, let us make it clear what is <u>not</u> *there*. In our passage, God says to Elijah,

"Get away from here." As long as you are satisfied with *here*, you'll never find that special place of fellowship and protection that Jesus welcomes His beloved to experience.

If there are times in your life when you just want to run, you are a candidate for *there*. But before you can approach the stairs of His quiet assurance, you must abandon the complacency and habits that hold you back. Your *here* may be a denominational preference. It may be a false doctrinal paradigm. It may be some kind of family connection. Your *here* may be pressing you so much that you are afraid to go *there*. But I'm here to tell you that you can go *there* when you are fed up with *here*.

Where Your Heart Turns to the Eternal

Verse 3 goes on to say, "Get away from here and turn *eastward*" (emphasis added). I wanted to know what *eastward* meant. Was I in for a shock! The word *eastward* in Deuteronomy 33:27 reads: "The eternal God is your refuge, And underneath are the everlasting arms; He will thrust out the enemy from before you, And will say, 'Destroy!'" That word *eternal* in this verse is the same word translated *eastward* in 1 Kings 17:3.

There is not only the place you go when you are fed up with *here*! *There* is the place where your heart turns toward the eternal! *East* is the place in Scripture where the eternal God is, the place where the everlasting arms are. The *eastward* God—the *eternal* God—is your refuge! He'll say to the enemy from that place, "You're finished." Glory to God!

Where to Discover the Secret of Hidden Life

God told Elijah to "hide by the brook." It was in this private, alone time that God met him personally. *There* is where you have quiet moments with the Father and discover the secret of the hidden life.

Recently, a man asked me what my resources are for my sermons. "Where do you get your ideas?" he asked. It's true that I have a vast library, and I've read most of the books. I have computer aids that are valuable tools. However, I prepare my messages by looking at every word that proceeds out of the mouth of God! Many times, on Saturday especially, I'll hear God calling me down to meet Him in the small study in the basement of my home.

My wife Paulette understands this because she also hears God calling her at five o'clock in the morning! When I get up, more than likely I'll find her on the porch weeping with an open Bible. If it is winter, I'll find her sitting by the gas logs. That's one place that she regularly finds the secret place.

Colossians 3:3 says that you are dead and "your life is hidden with Christ in God." There is a hidden life. There is a secret place of the Most High. There is a place only you can go with God. Deuteronomy 29:29 says, "The secret things belong to the Lord our God, but those things which are revealed belong to us." That word *secret* is the same word translated *hide* in Colossians 3:2. There is a place where God will whisper His secrets in your ear. There is a place where the things unknown can be revealed to your heart and your soul.

A Place for a Psalmist

King David understood the value of a secret place. Read Psalm 17:8-9 carefully. "Keep me as the apple of Your eye; Hide me under the shadow of Your wings, From the wicked who oppress me, From my deadly enemies who surround me." When you are under attack, there is a hiding place. King David also wrote in Psalm 27:5, "For in the time of trouble He shall hide me in His pavilion; In the secret place of His tabernacle He shall hide me; He shall set me high upon a rock."

God looked at Elijah when everybody wanted to kill him, when the drought had come, when everything was wrong, and said, "Hide yourself." When the attacks of the enemy and the voices of darkness come against me, what a comfort to be able to go to the hiding place. My Heavenly Father picks me up and dusts me off and washes me clean again in His blood and strengthens me. He says, "You've been down, but I'm going to set you on the Rock of Ages."

Where Covenant Seals You

Elijah the prophet fled to the Brook Cherith. Some scholars have researched and been puzzled by the observance that there is no record of an actual "Brook Cherith." But a clue comes when we uncover what the word *Cherith* means. In Genesis 15:18, God came to Abram and said, "I want to cut a covenant with you." *Cherith Berith* in Hebrew means to cut a covenant. So, God lifted Elijah, and basically said, "Go to the brook where I cut a covenant." I believe from these clues that the brook was the Jabath, where Jacob wrestled with the angel. The Jabath was a rushing stream and a refreshing haven.

If you were to ride down the West Bank in Israel, you can look across the Jordan River and see Mount Gilead, the fertile area where Elijah hid himself. It's still fertile! There is still a river flowing.

You may say you are thirsty, failing of hope. It is time to remember that there is water coming off a mountain! A river flows from Calvary, all the way into your life!

Elijah got to the place of healing. He got to the place where the water flowed. He got to the place of anointing. He got to the place of covenant agreement. Isn't that where our hearts desire to go?

I'm glad to tell you that there is a secret place of the Most High! There is a baptism of the Holy Ghost! There is a secret and hidden life! It's real—not just something that great men of God from ages ago experienced, but something that can be yours now! You see, the secret place is not something; it is Someone. You can flee to Him.

Where Change Releases the Supernatural

It is in the mighty presence of God that supernatural change can occur! Look at 1 Kings 17:4. "And it will be that you shall drink from the brook, and I have commanded the ravens to feed you there."

It is significant that God chose ravens to be the delivery agents! The biblical illustrator T. Dewitt Talmadge has this comment on the raven:

Again this story of the text impresses me that relief came to the prophet with the most unexpected and seemingly impossible conveyance. If it had been a robin redbreast, or a musical meadowlark, or a meek turtledove, or even a sublime albatross that had brought the food to Elijah, it would not have been so surprising. But, no, it was a bird so fierce and so auspicious that we have fashioned one of our most forceful and repulsive words from it—ravenous.*

---

*T. Dewitt Talmadge, *The Bible Illustrator,* Joseph Exell, ed., 1887, rep. Baker Book House, electronic version © 2002 AGES and Biblesoft, Inc.

Basically, the raven of Elijah was a buzzard! That particular bird has a passion for picking out the eyes of men and animals. It loves to maul the sick and dying. It swallows with a disgusting gurgle everything it can put its beak on. Yet, all the food that Elijah gets for six months or a year is to be brought to him by this dirty birdie! The laws given to Israel dictated that the raven was unclean meat, and stated that if you even touched anything a raven had touched, you would be unclean for a whole day! And yet, God looked at his number one prophet, Elijah, a man who was under the law, and God basically said, "If you think it's going to be like it's always been, you are wrong. I'm going to break the spirit of legalism."

I recently received a speaking invitation from a man who wrote, "I've got to ask you some questions. When you got the baptism of the Holy Ghost, did you speak in tongues right then? Because if you didn't, I just don't believe that what you've got is real." The man had twenty questions for me before he was ready to invite me to speak at his church! Let me tell you how I respond to that. "Thank you for your invitation. You'll be more comfortable with somebody else, because I don't have a God who would be locked in a Baptist box, an Assembly of God box, a Church of God box, or a Catholic box."

If Elijah had asked twenty questions, it would have meant his starvation! Can you imagine if Elijah had said, "Well, I tell you one thing, I'm not going to eat anything that these old buzzards have touched! I'm not going to touch unclean food! I must not have heard from God!" He would have died in the famine.

Of course, not only did Elijah have to be changed, but God had to redirect the raven as well! By nature, ravens scavenge and eat meat—they don't carry it to somebody else! Even today, God can change the hearts of the enemies of Christ to further the work of the kingdom! Listen again to Talmadge's thoughts on this over a hundred years ago:

> You think some great-hearted, generous person is going to come along and sign the back of your check, or that he will go security for you in some great enterprise. No, he will not. God will open the heart of some reprobate toward you. Your relief will come from the most unexpected quarter. The providence that seemed ominous will be to you more than which seemed auspicious. It will not be the

finch with a breast and wing dashed with white and brown and chestnut. It will be an ugly raven. Children of God, get up out of your despondency. The Lord has never had so many ravens as He has this morning.

Dr. Robert Schuller tells of the time when he and his congregation were trying to pay off the Crystal Cathedral. They had every building program. They had every fund-raiser. They prayed. But still they were falling short. He didn't know what to do. Late one Saturday night he was praying and weeping. He said, "Lord, I don't know what we're going to do. We can't make the next payment."

Suddenly, his phone rang. It was Frank Sinatra. He said, "Dr. Schuller, I've been watching you on TV for years. I've never done anything for you. Could you use $8 million?" That was how much they owed. God does the supernatural to release His provision in your life. God can bring it from unusual sources!

Just remember, the raven didn't want to carry meat for someone else, but had to do it. God commanded it. Do you understand that God can even influence lost people? God is in charge! We must understand that.

There is the hand of providence.

There is the power of the Holy Spirit.

There is where bushes burn and nations get set free, when prophets will listen.

There is where we are led by the still waters and He restores our soul.

There is the secret place of the Most High.

There is the Ark when the storms are washing away everything around the world.

There is where Jesus retreated in the night when He prayed His way to Calvary.

There is that heavenly place found by a man Paul knew who was caught up into the third heaven and saw things not lawful to be uttered.

There is where you're invited, if you are willing to die to self; if you are fed up with here; if you are ready to turn your heart toward the eternal; if you are ready to discover the secret of the hidden life; if you are ready to drink out of the covenant flow;—if you are ready to change.

Maybe you are ready to change because you have a son or daughter or grandchild who is in trouble and you need to see the hand of God. Per-haps you are looking in the face of an illness and know you can't do any-thing about it. It could be you find yourself in the middle of a problem and feel the crushing weight, realizing you cannot handle it alone.

One day you are going to get sick and tired of *here* and you're going to say, "Oh, God, get me *there!*" You have access today by faith to the presence of the Lord Jesus Christ. There is a place!

Chapter 4

Stop Running, Start Climbing!

The movie *Thelma and Louise* presented a parable of human drama and tragedy. In a desire to flee from abuse and resulting violence, these two women ran from their past. Pursued by authorities, their behavior escalated from harmless pranks into criminal acts. The movie ends with the two women hurtling to their deaths as they drive their car over the edge of the Grand Canyon. Their attempts to run from a past life in order to control their future culminated in the ultimate end for both of them.

Most of us as believers tend to take control of our own lives after conversion. Instead of growing more passionately in love with Jesus, we become practical and predictable. Soon, our hot hearts cool to a Laodicean lukewarm state that is tasteless and safely offends no one. We find people like Mary of Bethany, who weep and wash Jesus' feet with their tears, embarrassingly emotional.

Sadly, we now treat Christianity as something to fit neatly into our day planners, primarily an hour or two on Sunday. During the rest of our week, we are in pursuit of our own interests. I call this a "high-speed race to nowhere" or "running from the stairs."

There is an Old Testament character who fits perfectly into our twenty-first-century scene. His very name, Jacob, means "wheeler-dealer." He was shrewd and crafty, using his skill to steal his own brother's blessing and birthright. His life is a constant chase, with Yahweh in hot pursuit of His fleeing child.

Jacob was always in a hurry. If you look at his early life, it resembles a spiritual yo-yo. On one life-changing journey, Jacob turned aside to rest from his travels, using a stone for a pillow, and had visions of stairs leading to heaven! He saw angels dance and come and go upon those stairs. In that supernatural encounter, Yahweh promised Jacob manifold blessings.

> So he came to a certain place and stayed there all night, because the sun had set. And he took one of the stones of that place and put it at his head, and he lay down in that place to sleep. Then he dreamed, and behold, a ladder was set up on the earth, and its top reached to heaven; and there the angels of God were ascending and descending on it.
>
> And behold, the Lord stood above it and said: "I am the Lord God of Abraham your father and the God of Isaac; the land on which you lie I will give to you and your descendants. Also your descendants shall be as the dust of the earth; you shall spread abroad to the west and the east, to the north and the south; and in you and in your seed all the families of the earth shall be blessed.
>
> Genesis 28:11-14

In spite of this dynamic experience, Jacob did not stop his hurried lifestyle. Like most of us, he had a schedule, appointments, and agenda of his own. And so, Yahweh again sought to get his attention, this time literally wrestling him to the ground, crippling him in order to bless him (Ge 32:24-32).

This second face-to-face encounter resulted in Jacob receiving a new name, Israel, which means "prince of God." Carnal aggressiveness had to be broken in the busy but backslidden Jacob. Chastened and changed, Israel limped away from his divine encounter.

Unbelievably, soon Israel slipped back to his old "Jacob" patterns! Like so many of us, he refused to take the ladder offered to climb into God's presence. Before long, Jacob's family faced disaster. His daughter became sexually active and his sons killed hundreds of young men. Into this horrific scene, God again summoned Jacob to return to the place of his first visions.

> Then God said to Jacob, "Arise, go up to Bethel and dwell there; and make an altar there to God, who appeared to you when you fled from the face of Esau your brother."

acob said to his household and to all who were with him,
ay the foreign gods that are among you, purify yourselves,
hange your garments. Then let us arise and go up to Bethel;
will make an altar there to God, who answered me in the day
my distress and has been with me in the way which I have gone."
they gave Jacob all the foreign gods which were in their hands,
and the earrings which were in their ears; and Jacob hid them under
the terebinth tree which was by Shechem.

And they journeyed, and the terror of God was upon the cities
that were all around them, and they did not pursue the sons of Jacob. So Jacob came to Luz (that is, Bethel), which is in the land of
Canaan, he and all the people who were with him. And he built an
altar there and called the place El Bethel, because there God appeared to him when he fled from the face of his brother.

Genesis 35:1-7

On all these occasions, Jacob ran headlong into God. He literally stum-
bled onto the stairs! How sad that so many of us are too busy, too preoc-
cupied, and in too big of a hurry! Because of our mad rush, we miss
angelic intervention, burning bushes, supernatural visitations, and experi-
ences of divine love.

Doves, Not Chickens!

We are summoned to let go of a life of running, wrestling, and failing,
and to grasp hold of a life that has wings! We can move to a higher plane!
"O my dove, that art in the clefts of the rock, in the secret places of the
stairs, let me see thy countenance, let me hear thy voice; for sweet is thy
voice, and thy countenance is comely" (Song 2:14 KJV). This verse shows
the Bridegroom, that picture of Jesus, calling the church a "dove." In Hebrew, this is a reference to the turtledove. The Middle Eastern doves were
wild and elusive. They had a loving nature and lived in pairs. They were
quite beautiful in their plumage and were treasured by the people.

The dove preferred the wilds to the populated places. The poor used
these wild birds for their Temple sacrifice. A poor family would capture
two lovebirds and carry them to the priest. These pets then would be of-

fered to God. One would die, and the other
blood of its mate upon its wings and soar u

This represented the death of all othe
the presence of our Lord. He is to be the su
When Jesus ascended back to heaven, He open
blood.

Can you imagine a poor leper having been healed, w
fice being made on his behalf? He sees the bird killed and n
kled on the wings of the living bird. He watches the living bird
to the skies. Hear him shout, "By the blood of another, I now live, a
go into the presence of God!"

Jacob a Dove

Like the wild dove, Jacob had finally been captured by God, and found
his purpose and destiny as the patriarch of God's nation, Israel. We, too,
can find our destiny and be captured and enraptured in the Father's presence. We are summoned to be alone with God so that we can commune
with Him. We are summoned to the cleft of the Rock in the high places.
The place to which we are called is high but also holy. Just like the Holy of
Holies in the tabernacle housed the presence of God, we are summoned
not to a church building but to a personal audience with Jesus.

Psalms 24:3-6 speaks to that generation that desires to seek the awesome presence of Jesus:

Who may ascend into the hill of the Lord?
    Or who may stand in His holy place?
He who has clean hands and a pure heart,
    Who has not lifted up his soul to an idol,
    Nor sworn deceitfully.
He shall receive blessing from the Lord,
    And righteousness from the God of his salvation.
This *is* Jacob, the generation of those who seek Him,
    Who seek Your face.

Psalm 24:3-6

Who can go to this secret place? Who can know the secret of the stairs that lead to communion with God? It will be those whose inner life (the heart) is right as well as the outward life (their hands). Thank God we are washed in His blood! We have received Jesus' righteousness for the filthy rags of our own righteousness. Our pride and vanity must bite the dust if we are to ascend the hill of the Lord. Every substitute love standing as an idol must be ripped from our hearts.

Hope for Our Generation

There is an urgent and comforting lesson in this choice. Yes, indeed, the climb toward intimacy with God is made through the awesome gift of God's grace. Grace is God's favor for the disfavored! Grace allows the Jacobs of today to climb to the status of Israel, a prince of God. This is the man whose twelve sons would become the nation, Israel.

Yes, all that Jacob was promised is ours. We too have stairs to climb. We have access to God's presence. We can ascend the hill of the Lord. He has invited us to come. We must quit our running, our wrestling, and our wandering, and come home. He awaits us on the stairs.

When I was in seminary, I remember facing a particularly trying time of deep discouragement. A dear friend named Bobby Welch grabbed me and said, "Ronnie, let's pray!" Being in the hallway at the time, he looked around for a more private spot and steered me under the staircase. As he began to pray, I felt the Holy Spirit begin to lift me out of my despair.

That place under those apartment stairs became a secret place of prayer where God was able to shape my life.

The Lord is very near. Like Jacob, you may be running hard in life. As near as your breath is the God you hunger for. He is waiting to drop the stairs in front of you. You must stop your running and wrestling. You must get alone with Him. In that secret place, He will show up, bushes will burn, angels will operate, His word will be clear, and His love will wash over you. He is waiting for you, calling you to that rendezvous at His staircase.

THE UPWARD CLIMB

Chapter 5

Climbing Out of the Valley

David was a man who pursued the very heart of God. David was different than others. He was odd in appearance from most other Israelites. In a dark-eyed, dark-skinned culture, he had "bright eyes" and was "ruddy and of a fair countenance" (1 Sa 17:42 KJV). David—the blue-eyed, pale-skinned redhead!

David's family thought him different and tried to hide him in ways. When Samuel showed up at the house of Jesse to anoint the second king of Israel, Jesse didn't mention his youngest son David at first. David the "different" one was safely hidden in the field taking care of the sheep.

In spite of his environment of prejudice and sibling angst, David had learned that he was never alone. As a shepherd himself, he learned, "The Lord is my shepherd" (Psalm 23:1). David became a worshipper and a lover of the Lord Jesus out in those fields. God became the greatest desire of his young heart!

Long evenings of solitude under the starry heavens taught David that he was never alone! What may have appeared to many to be a crude country life was far more. Every star above his head sang of the love of God. In the darkness of night, David's soul glowed with the light of God's presence. "The Lord is my light and my salvation; Whom shall I fear? The Lord is the strength of my life; Of whom shall I be afraid?" (Ps 27:1).

When David trudged up the hills of Judea, the simple trek was transformed by the presence of God. "I will lift up my eyes to the hills—From whence comes my help?" (Ps 121:1). Suddenly, his trail upward became a pilgrim journey into the secret place!

Every outcropping of rock became the "shadow of the Almighty." Even gurgling streams carried echoes of heaven. David practiced the presence of God and learned the skills of leader and shepherd as He worshipped and communed with Jehovah.

His most famous work, Psalm 23, sums up David's extraordinary wilderness experience with God. David's intimacy with his Creator propelled him forward to courageous leadership and fame. His rock-solid assurance of God's faithfulness sent him to fell Goliath, protected him from Saul's fury, elevated him to leadership, attracted others to follow him, and finally took him to the throne.

When you read Psalm 23, it has about it the lyric of a lover. David knew God as Lord, Yahweh, the Great I Am, and the God of covenant! The young shepherd boy realized God was the Shepherd of Israel, the Provider and Protector. This future king may have been walking in the wilderness, but he inhabited the house of God!

David learned that God's presence was brought on by praise. As he cared for his sheep, he learned to conquer fear. He faced and killed both a lion and a bear while tending those sheep. Even as he stood guard over his flock, he came to understand that God was closely by his side.

Worship on the Stairs

When your problems rise up before you like a Goliath, what can you do? You can worship and have faith in God! Your worship will lift you above that which had towered over you. As you sing and commune with God, you ascend the stairs into His place of fellowship.

You may come from a dysfunctional family like David. You may be different and even feel like an outcast. Take heart! You can turn your solitude into a sanctuary and turn your loneliness into life! Remember, David received the anointing of God to lead the people, different as he was. Goliath could not kill him. The jealous King Saul could not destroy him. The Philistines could not buy him off. Hell could not stop him. Even sin could not finish him, for he knew the power of God's forgiveness.

Love Song to God

David sang out to the God of his salvation, not to gain anything for himself—he didn't want wealth, titles, or land. His whole desire was to know the heart of God. He wrote,

One thing I have desired of the Lord,
>   That will I seek:
>   That I may dwell in the house of the Lord
>   All the days of my life,
>   To behold the beauty of the Lord,
>   And to inquire in His temple.
For in the time of trouble
>   He shall hide me in His pavilion;
>   In the secret place of His tabernacle
>   He shall hide me;
>   He shall set me high upon a rock.
And now my head shall be lifted up above my enemies all around
>   me;
>   Therefore I will offer sacrifices of joy in His tabernacle;
>   I will sing, yes, I will sing praises to the Lord.
Hear, O Lord, when I cry with my voice!
>   Have mercy also upon me, and answer me.
When You said, "Seek My face,"
>   My heart said to You, "Your face, Lord, I will seek."
Do not hide Your face from me;
>   Do not turn Your servant away in anger;
>   You have been my help;
>   Do not leave me nor forsake me,
>   O God of my salvation.

Psalm 27:4-9

David longed to live in the presence of the Lord. At this point, no temple had been built, so in this Scripture he isn't referring to church attendance; rather, he refers to the hours spent in the secret place of the stairs, the private time with he and God alone.

Above All Trouble

David was seeking God's presence. He wanted to gaze on the beauty of the Lord! He wanted to pray to the living God. He wanted protection and immunity from His enemies.

"For in the time of trouble He shall hide me in His pavilion; In the secret place of His tabernacle He shall hide me; He shall set me high upon a rock" (Ps 27:5).

There David sang praises to the Lord while lifted above those who would destroy him. David sought the face of God. David was passionately obsessed with knowing God. God's face turned toward a person signalled unparalleled blessing and power.

Even in the time of failure and sin, David fled to the Lord. After his affair with Bathsheba, the resulting fallout of her pregnancy, and the ordered death of her husband Uriah, David fled to the Lord. Both Psalm 32 and Psalm 51 were songs written by a broken David confessing his sins to God. His appeal for "tender mercies" grabbed the heart of God and David was forgiven and restored.

Running headlong into the realization of God's amazing love is a transforming event! Author and former Franciscan monk, Brennan Manning, writes of such an experience for him at the end of a private spiritual retreat.

Jesus removed the shroud of perfectionistic performance and now, forgiven and free, I ran home. For I *knew* that I knew that Someone was there for me. Gripped in the depth of my soul, tears streaming down my cheeks, I internalized and finally felt all the words I have written and spoken about stubborn, unrelenting Love. That morning I understood that the words are but straw compared to the Reality. I leaped from simply becoming the teacher of God's love to becoming Abba's delight. I said goodbye to feeling frightened and said *shalom* to feeling safe" (*Abba's Child*, NavPress, 2002).

As we take steps into God's presence, we discover that there is pardon and forgiveness. There is a place on the stairs for those that fail. In the honesty of confession we find a open door to His presence.

Chapter 6

Climbing on the Promises

The hot Nigerian sun beat down upon our team as we prepared to leave for the airport. I had been in Africa for a preaching crusade, and though the time had come to leave our host pastor, we took a moment to pray and rejoice with Dr. Ezeh before departing.

The prayers for provision for our journey still rang in our ears as we walked into the local airport, only to discover in shock that our flight to Lagos was cancelled! This news had serious implications! If we did not make it to Lagos that very day, we would miss our flight out of Africa, and our return to the United States would be delayed four days until the next available outbound flight!

Some quick scrambling and calculating revealed that our only hope was to make a mad three-and-a-half-hour dash to catch a different flight from the airport in Port Harcourt, but we had to hustle to find appropriate vehicles and leave immediately, as we had only a fifteen-minute time margin!

The situation was made even more complicated by the fact that gasoline was scarce in Nigeria at the time. A two-week shutdown of the refineries had left the nation in the grip of a fuel shortage. Many gas stations were closed or were rationing fuel.

An hour into our drive, I noticed that the gas gauge in our borrowed vehicle registered below empty. I leaned forward and asked our Nigerian driver, Brother A.G. Bright, if his fuel gauge was broken.

"No, my brother," he answered, "but God will provide, for we prayed for mercy on this journey. Also, you and Dr. Ezeh are God's men. He will surely see us through."

It is difficult to admit, but my faithless soul was not comforted. I immediately had visions of our team stranded with our vehicles in the middle of the sweltering Nigerian jungle! I could imagine rebels and robbers taking us captive!

Suddenly, my driver began to sing praises to God. Others in the car joined in, but still I fretted, sure that any second I would hear the car motor grind to a halt. After another hour of driving, we came upon a crossroads, and a gas station stood at the intersection. As we pulled in, we could see that it indeed was open for business! In fact, we soon found out that the proprietor of the station had been closed for a week, so his supply was not exhausted, and actually had just reopened as we pulled up!

A smiling A.G. Bright looked at me and said, "See, Pastor Phillips, God always takes care of His servants. You are in favor with God!"

What a powerful lesson! Again I learned that God responds not to my fretful desperation, but to a faithful man's passionate praise.

Spiritual Insiders

God is looking for some worshippers who are ready to press on for more. There is much about God we do not know. But God wants to reveal Himself and His plan to those who are willing to be His intimate friends. "The secret things belong to the Lord our God, but those things which are revealed belong to us and to our children forever, that we may do all the words of this law" (De 29:29).

God reveals truths to those who will discipline themselves to climb up to Him on the stairs of faith. Abraham discovered this, for he became a "spiritual insider" with God. God called him "friend." When God was about to unleash judgment on Sodom and Gomorrah, He let Abraham in on that plan. "And the Lord said, "Shall I hide from Abraham what I am doing, since Abraham shall surely become a great and mighty nation, and all the nations of the earth shall be blessed in him?" (Ge 18:17-18).

Where is the company of men and women who are willing to scale the stairs to His presence to find out what His heart is concerning our world? Where are the intercessors who can go in face-to-face with God and plead the cause of lost humanity?

Seeking God's Face

In the Old Covenant, only the high priest could access the Holy of Holies that housed the divine presence of God. In the New Covenant, we all have access to the stairs. Here we behold the face of our Lord. Too often, we act as though we seek God's face, when honestly we only seek His hand. We try to pull at His purse strings instead of crying after His presence! But God only releases provision on those who are hungry for Him. This passage reveals that blessing:

> And the Lord spoke to Moses, saying: "Speak to Aaron and his sons, saying, 'This is the way you shall bless the children of Israel. Say to them:
> The Lord bless you and keep you;
> The Lord make His face shine upon you,
>   And be gracious to you;
> The Lord lift up His countenance upon you,
>   And give you peace."
> So they shall put My name on the children of Israel, and I will bless them.
>
> Numbers 6:22-27

The seeker's blessing is full of promise. Yahweh told Moses to release this blessing through Aaron and the priestly line to all of the people. They were to speak God's name, which is Yahweh, the Great I Am, upon the people. In that name is unlimited blessing, immunity and protection, and God's favor and presence!

Whatever you need, the God of the stairs can give you! In that secret place, you discover His name is not "Thou Shalt Not" but "I Am." He is the God whose "No" means "Don't hurt yourself" and whose "Yes" means "Help yourself to My provisions!"

God Still Speaks

God wants to reveal marvelous secrets of His kingdom. Are you one of the few who will wait on Him and listen? We are promised, "The secret of the Lord is with those who fear Him, and He will show them his covenant" (Ps 25:14).

As we bow in fear and reverence before Him, He will show us all the covenant promises made to us in Christ Jesus. The Bible is filled with mysteries that God is still fulfilling. God desires to reveal to us all that is ours in the New Covenant. What did God promise through this covenant? Our covenant promises us many benefits including healing, deliverance, freedom, and prosperity.

Secret Riches

Isaiah 45 celebrated the release of Israel from bondage by the anointed leader, Cyrus of Persia. Cyrus did not know that he was God's instrument to bless His people.

Listen to this first promise of material provision: "I will give you the treasures of darkness And hidden riches of secret places, That you may know that I, the Lord, Who call you by your name, Am the God of Israel" (Is 45:3).

One of the blessings of finding that secret place of the presence of God is that we become partakers in God's promise to provide our material needs. When we enter the secret place of the stairs, Yahweh loads us with benefits and blessing. The promise of showers of blessing comes many times in Scripture, including this verse in Isaiah. "Rain down, you heavens, from above, And let the skies pour down righteousness; Let the earth open, let them bring forth salvation, And let righteousness spring up together. I, the Lord, have created it" (45:8).

Not only does God promise to pour out salvation upon the whole earth and maintain a plan to touch the world but God also begs us to pray. "Thus says the Lord, The Holy One of Israel, and his Maker: "Ask Me of things to come concerning My sons; And concerning the work of My hands, you command Me" (Is 45:11).

Supply from His Hand

He invites us to command His blessing on all the works of His hand. Then Yahweh promises us the riches of the world.

Thus says the Lord:

> "The labor of Egypt and merchandise of Cush
> And of the Sabeans, men of stature,
> Shall come over to you, and they shall be yours;
> They shall walk behind you,
> They shall come over in chains;
> And they shall bow down to you.
> They will make supplication to you, saying,
> 'Surely God is in you,
> And there is no other;
> There is no other God."

Isaiah 45:14

In the Hidden Place

Our God does not show His secrets to just anyone. Instead, the prophet tells us that our God is often hidden in His plan and purpose. "Truly You are God, who hide Yourself, O God of Israel, the Savior!" (Is 45:15).

Sometimes God speaks to us in the hidden place of the stairs for no reason. "I have not spoken in secret, In a dark place of the earth; I did not say to the seed of Jacob, 'Seek Me in vain'; I, the Lord, speak righteousness, I declare things that are right" (Is 45:19).

Your time spent seeking God will not be without result! It is not a waste of time to spend time in His secret place! Those who seek Him will hear His voice. God will reveal His riches to you as you get alone with Him and seek His face. Once there, tell your Heavenly Father what you need.

Is the gas tank of your life on empty? His provision is abundant and miraculous. In His service, at the feet of Jesus, you will never find yourself in want!

Chapter 7

Upward Through the Tears

The phone rang as I stepped out of the shower early that morning, and as I picked up the receiver, I heard the voice of a stranger on the other end say, "Mr. Phillips, your wife Paulette has been in a little fender-bender."

I dressed quickly and jumped in the car, following the directions of the caller to find the accident scene. As I crested a hill on the main highway, I was unprepared for what I saw. Even through the drizzling rain, I spotted my wife's little convertible, now a twisted mass of metal! An ambulance stood waiting, and workers were trying to free her from the wreckage. The smell of gasoline was heavy in the air.

I tried to get close to the car but was held back by emergency workers. I was frustrated, knowing she must be desperately hurt, and yet I was unable to offer comfort. However, God had provided someone at the scene to do that for me. A fireman, at the risk of his own life due to the potential for an explosion, popped out a window and climbed in next to Paulette. He covered her with an asbestos blanket, held on to her and spoke life into her, watching her carefully and keeping her talking to be sure she wasn't falling into deep shock.

It was twenty-five agonizing minutes before the firemen and the Jaws of Life would free her from the car. And we didn't know it then, but it would be six months before her crumpled body would allow her to return to a normal life.

As I ran to Paulette's side while they hurried her stretcher toward the ambulance, I remembered clearly hearing her say, "Thank you, Lord!" I know that in the midst of that tragedy, God was there. In addition, He provided a wonderful young, Christian fireman whose presence comforted my wife in that dark hour. His heroic presence was the touch of God. She felt carried in the Father's arms.

The Way of Tears

When tragedy strikes, we find ourselves in need of the assurance of God's presence more than ever before. It is no coincidence that our ascent into the most secret place of the heavenly stairs can occur in times of great heartache and tragedy. Tears have a way of driving us from ourselves to Him. Who hasn't cried out in the dark night of the soul for solace that only can come from Jesus? Expect to find the stairs into His secret place stained with the tears of thousands of heartbroken saints before you.

Isaiah, the court prophet, cousin and confidant to King Uzziah, thought he had it all. His cousin King, although a leper, had given the nation peace and hope. Isaiah's own ministry was one that sternly laid down the law to God's wayward people. He had angered them, calling them stubborn, ungrateful children, and even went as far as to compare them to "rotten, stinking grapes!"

Surely God was pleased with Isaiah's obedience in ministry. And He surely had the ear and heart of his cousin, King Uzziah.

Here I interrupt the story so you will see that Isaiah is like many of us. When you read the first five chapters of Isaiah, though inspired, you feel something missing in Isaiah's life. There is a lack of hope and only a vague hinting of what God is actually up to. Isaiah 6 gives us the turning point— an amazing "alone" experience with God that is vivid and clear.

After Isaiah's dear cousin king died suddenly, Isaiah felt his life collapsing. The hope that had sustained him, and the promise of ministry in a peaceful Jerusalem that kept his eyes looking ahead, seemed to evaporate. Tragedy is like that. Normally, it will either drive us to God or cause us to run away from Him.

But Isaiah made the boldest decision any prophet ever made. He decided to charge into God's presence! Isaiah turned purposefully toward the temple of Solomon, the three-room structure that housed God's presence. Beyond the outer court, beyond the candlelit Holy Place, Isaiah knew there hung a thick veil. Beyond that veil, God promised to be present. However, the rules were clear—anyone who went past that veil, other than the High Priest, would be struck down by God! And even the High Priest could only enter The Holy of Holies once a year!

Live or Die

Isaiah came to the place of absolute self-abandonment, just as a seeker of the stairs today must approach God. Death no longer mattered to Isaiah. He pushed his way past quiet worshippers and astounded priests to get to God. Isaiah needed help and hope, and had come to the end of his own resources. He was now a candidate for a miracle. He pressed past the veil into the Holy of Holies. The fearful protesters behind Isaiah no doubt backed away in fear, sure that this crazed man was walking into certain death.

There in the Holy of Holies, lit by only the Shekinah glory of God, Isaiah did die, in a sense. He died to himself and all his own ambitions! In this bold step, I believe Isaiah gave up on Isaiah! He met Yahweh, and nothing else mattered. God was in that place, high and lifted up with His unmatched glory trailing behind Him, like the train of royal robes billowing behind a sovereign. Angelic worshippers surrounded the throne crying "Holy!" The place shook with the voice of the angels.

In the year that King Uzziah died, I saw the Lord sitting on a throne, high and lifted up, and the train of His robe filled the temple. Above it stood seraphim; each one had six wings: with two he covered his face, with two he covered his feet, and with two he flew. And one cried to another and said:
"Holy, holy, holy is the Lord of hosts;
The whole earth is full of His glory!"
And the posts of the door were shaken by the voice of him who cried out, and the house was filled with smoke.

Isaiah 6:1-4

Isaiah had no choice but to die to his flesh and ambitions. "Woe is me . . ." he cried, in an expression that could be also translated, "I am doomed!"

He looked at the evil society around him and saw that even his own mouth, the mouth of a man of God, was unclean. Angels brought cleansing fire to touch his preaching lips, and his life was transformed. Soon he heard the voice of God crying for volunteers to carry His message. "Here am I, send me!" cried the transformed Isaiah.

So I said:
"Woe is me, for I am undone!
Because I am a man of unclean lips,
And I dwell in the midst of a people of unclean lips;
For my eyes have seen the King, The Lord of hosts."
Then one of the seraphim flew to me, having in his hand a live coal which he had taken with the tongs from the altar. And he touched my mouth with it, and said:
"Behold, this has touched your lips;
Your iniquity is taken away,
And your sin purged."
Also I heard the voice of the Lord, saying:
"Whom shall I send, And who will go for Us?"
Then I said, "Here am I! Send me.

Isaiah 6:5-8

No man can see the Lord and continue living like nothing ever happened! No, the old life will be burned away and a new life will begin. The New Testament puts it this way:

I have been crucified with Christ; it is no longer I who live, but Christ lives in me; and the *life* which I now live in the flesh I live by faith in the Son of God, who loved me and gave Himself for me.

Galatians 2:20

And those who are Christ's have crucified the flesh with its passions and desires.

Galatians 5:24

But God forbid that I should boast except in the cross of our Lord Jesus Christ, by whom the world has been crucified to me, and I to the world.

Galatians 6:14

In the secret place of God, we come to the end of ourselves. We come as a bride to take on Jesus' name and nature. When we are willing to die daily, Jesus says to us:

> If anyone desires to come after Me, let him deny himself, and take up his cross daily, and follow Me. For whoever desires to save his life will lose it, but whoever loses his life for My sake will save it.
>
> Luke 9:23-24

Isaiah Transformed

You need only turn the pages of the rest of Isaiah's book to discover what happened to him after his life-transforming experience. He now could see beyond this earth and beyond time into the purposes of God. New revelation began to pour, with prophecies that had eternal significance and weight:

–A virgin-born King was coming—"call His name Immanuel" (Is 7:14)

–He would be God come to earth—"the government will be upon His shoulder" (Is 9:6)

–He would be Wonderful!—(Is 9:6)

–He would die for His people —"He was wounded for our transgressions . . . he was led as a lamb to the slaughter" (Is 53:5, 7).

Isaiah saw the same One we will see if we are willing to follow Him up the sacred stairs into the secret place. Isaiah saw Jesus! Jesus dried Isaiah's tears, changed His life, gave Him revelation knowledge, and showed him His love.

When you go to the stairs, the same blessings are yours. God's life will kill your flesh then fill your life. His word will come alive. He will make you an insider and show you things to come.

Chapter 8

Onward Through the Challenge

People of "the stairs" affect the leadership and destiny of nations and generations. No matter the life you've lived before approaching the stairs, your destiny forever changes as you set your foot into His holy presence.

You may have read of a lowly tinker named John. This man had so little education that he didn't really learn to read and write until he was married! He had grown up godless and careless, and his terrifying ways and blasphemous speech frightened his community. But the outward hardness concealed an inward hunger for God, and John the tinker soon found himself drawn into a life-changing, sin-breaking encounter with God.

"I never saw such heights and depths in grace, and love, and mercy," he later wrote. "Now was God and Christ continually before my face . . . The glory of the holiness of God did at this time break me to pieces."*

John's encounter on the stairs would bring him to begin preaching in power, and many in his community came to Christ. His message was unpopular for the time, however, and he was imprisoned in a filthy jail for several years. But Christians through the centuries have been transfixed by the writings of this man, for while in that prison, John Bunyan picked up his pen and wrote the immortal allegory *Pilgrim's Progress*. The work stands today as one of the most read books in the world, having changed countless lives with its stirring picture of a lost soul finding salvation.

Mysterious Prophet

Looking further back in history, we find a Biblical figure exploding into history like a holy hurricane. Take a closer look at the prophet Elijah the

---

*John Bunyan, *Grace Abounding to the Chief of Sinners*, ch. VI.

Tishbite of Gilead, who, similar to the mysterious Melchizedek of Genesis, roars onto the scene like a lion. The Bible doesn't tell us exactly what his roots were or where he was trained. He had no human lineage to recommend him, no seminary degree to qualify him, and no resume to promote him. From where did this man with a message come? The Scripture gives us strong hints that this man came white hot with the glory of God from that secret place we call the "stairs."

In the days preceding Elijah's arrival, Israel knew prosperity but had forgotten God, much like our day. While ripe with material possessions, the nation withered under the wicked reign of Ahab and Jezebel. As I discussed in chapter three, Elijah quickly got the nation's attention—and their fury—when he announced the coming of a yearlong drought.

How did he know about this coming disaster? How did he find the boldness to make such a prophetic utterance? People in that day no doubt wondered, "Who is this strange, rough man wearing the mantle of a prophet? Who dared name him 'Elijah,' which means 'Yahweh is God'?" There was confidence and boldness in this prophet's words: "As the Lord God of Israel lives, before whom I stand, there shall not be dew nor rain these years, except at my word" (1 Ki 17:1).

The truth was that Elijah staked his message on the very life of Yahweh! He boldly confronted the wicked Ahab to his face. Elijah saw himself standing in the presence of Yahweh God even though his feet were planted firmly on the earth. He equated his prophetic announcement to the very word of the Living God.

How was such fearless ministry possible? How can we reach a level of authority that shakes heaven and earth? If we look again at Scripture, we discover this ragged prophet's secret: knowing how to get to God on the stairs.

Elijah's Hiding Place

Elijah's spiritual origins were not geographical, and you cannot find a religious organization that sent him forth. His origins were not horizontal, of the earth, but vertical, of heaven. He arose from the same place every true man or woman of God must arise. Elijah came on the scene from the secret place of the Lord. Having been hidden away with the Lord at the

Brook Cherith, he knew what the Lord was doing. The hiding place with God cannot be found on a map. It is wherever a person can run into the secret place with God and know Him intimately.

God speaks His secrets to those who draw near. He provides a place of keeping and protection for those He calls "the apple of my eye."

A Man Like Us

Elijah was an ordinary man who became extraordinary when he chose the presence of God over the company of men! Elijah's word directed by God controlled nature, shook kingdoms, and brought life. James tells us that this man was like us. "Elijah was a man with a nature like ours, and he prayed earnestly that it would not rain; and it did not rain on the land for three years and six months" (5:17). Elijah's secret can be your secret! The difference in his life was the time spent in the company of Yahweh!

Elijah was in covenant with Yahweh, and he only moved when Yahweh gave the order. Too many of us move then cry out to God. He is looking for a people that will lie at His feet and not move until He moves, like Ruth did when she sought Boaz as her kinsman-redeemer.

Signs Follow

Elijah blazes a trail of obedience, and in his wake came powerful miracles. On to Zaraphath he goes, following the order of God. There he meets a widow with a young son, whom God had instructed to feed and house the prophet. God had to do a miracle of provision for her in order to care for His servant. When Elijah first approached her for food, she replied,

So she said, "As the Lord your God lives, I do not have bread, only a handful of flour in a bin, and a little oil in a jar; and see, I am gathering a couple of sticks that I may go in and prepare it for myself and my son, that we may eat it, and die."

And Elijah said to her, "Do not fear; go and do as you have said, but make me a small cake from it first, and bring it to me; and afterward make some for yourself and your son. For thus says the Lord

God of Israel: 'The bin of flour shall not be used up, nor shall the jar of oil run dry, until the day the Lord sends rain on the earth.'"

So she went away and did according to the word of Elijah; and she and he and her household ate for many days. The bin of flour was not used up, nor did the jar of oil run dry, according to the word of the Lord which He spoke by Elijah.

1 Kings 17:12-16

Miraculous provision flowed from the word of God in Elijah. More testing would follow, as the widow's son grew sick and then dies, but Elijah trusted God's power over death. Yet another miracle occurs: "Then the Lord heard the voice of Elijah; and the soul of the child came back to him, and he revived. And Elijah took the child and brought him down from the upper room into the house, and gave him to his mother. And Elijah said, 'See, your son lives!' " (1 Ki 17:22-23).

Note the phrase, "the Lord heard the voice of Elijah." Why was God tuned to Elijah's cry? Because Elijah's voice was one that God knew well. It was the voice of one who knew the secret place of the stairs.

Fire from Heaven

After three years, Elijah sent word to Ahab, challenging the forces of hell to meet him on Mt. Carmel. The Lord was about to expose the false prophets of Baal, kick the foundation out from under the evil rule of Ahab and Jezebel, and break the drought by sending rain.

This man Elijah was ordinary, and yet he stood against the very forces of evil that governed a whole nation! After the prophets of Baal failed to produce fire from heaven for their altar, Elijah drenched his sacrifice, the wood, and the area surrounding the altar with water, then prayed, "'Hear me, O Lord, hear me, that this people may know that You are the Lord God, and that You have turned their hearts back to You again.' Then the fire of the Lord fell and consumed the burnt sacrifice, and the wood and the stones and the dust, and it licked up the water that was in the trench" (1 Ki 18:37-38).

Fire falls! Evil was routed! And in short order, the drought over the country was broken!

Our generation longs for rain also—the rain of renewal! Do we want revival today? Are we willing to confront evil, to hide ourselves, to risk our reputations? We too can call for the fire and loose the rain if we learn to hide ourselves in His secret place.

Back to the Stairs

So that we would really believe Elijah was an ordinary man with an extraordinary God, we are given another scene from his life. This man who could not be frightened by 450 prophets or a wicked king is suddenly turned into a coward by the threat of one woman, the notorious Jezebel. She represents control, especially control of God's men. Her spirit lives on in the New Testament where we find her spirit hindering the church.

> Nevertheless I have a few things against you, because you allow that woman Jezebel, who calls herself a prophetess, to teach and seduce My servants to commit sexual immorality and eat things sacrificed to idols.
>
> Revelation 2:20

Elijah runs from this woman into the wilderness of Beersheba. He has been away from the stairs too long! Now suffering from suicidal depression, he cries out to God, "It is enough! Now, Lord, take my life, for I am no better than my fathers!" (1 Ki 19:4).

But God still knew the voice of His child. God sent an angel to strengthen his servant, not just with words of peace and strength but also with practical supply for his physical needs. The food and drink the angel gave Elijah sustained him for 40 days! (1 Ki 19:5-8)

Elijah moved on to Arabia and climbed Mt. Horeb, or what we know as Sinai. He knew he had to return to the stairs. God asks him, "What are you doing here, Elijah?" (1 Ki 19:9).

Elijah was throwing himself a little pity party. In the middle of all that, God puts on a spectacular display of power. First came a windstorm, then an earthquake, then a fire. Yet God was not evident in those. But shortly, God came to Elijah in a "still, small voice." "And it was so, when Elijah heard it, that he wrapped his face in his mantle and went out and stood in the entrance of the cave. Suddenly a voice came to him, and said, "What are you doing here, Elijah?" (I Kings 19:13).

God went on to encourage Elijah with the word that he was not alone—He revealed the glad news that there were 7,000 more in Israel who had not given themselves over to worship of Baal!

In the passages that follow, we learn that God actually gave Elijah one of those 7,000 faithful godly men to be his companion. God introduced His two friends to each other. Elisha came to be a servant and to be mentored to eventually take Elijah's office.

Never Alone

Take comfort, my seeking, climbing friend! You are not alone! There are a symbolic 7000, a number of perfection and completeness, who are climbing with us. We shall meet each other on the stairs! Perhaps God may bring one of His faithful alongside to team up with you to finish your task.

Even in the absence of friends, God still will provide for you! When your spiritual tank is empty, angels will feed you until you get back to the stairs, and His Spirit will never leave you comfortless!

THE UPWARD
COMMUNION

Chapter 9

The Place Near Him

We have fast food and drive-throughs for almost any service. Instant banking, drive-through pharmacies, laundry drop-offs—everything is prepared in a hurry for our convenience!

Unfortunately, in our "have-it-now," instant society, we expect even spirituality to happen quickly. We want instant miracles, sudden breakthroughs, and smooth, problem-free lives.

I can imagine the day the first church installs a drive-through! You could zip your tithe or offering through a slot and receive in return your communion cup and a thin communion wafer. Then maybe a squirt of anointing oil shoots out and a mechanical hand taps you on the head for a blessing as you prepare to drive away! If that seems unspiritual and far-fetched, take a look what is an all-too-common expectation at church: the hope that an altar service will provide a quick fix for all of our problems.

How often does our modern worship experience focus on our neediness rather than Jesus' majesty? We think that we can achieve instant intimacy with God with a quick experience at an altar. Jesus certainly wants to meet those needs, but the meeting of our needs is a by-product, not a goal, of worship.

The Father is seeking those who will worship Him in spirit and truth. "But the hour is coming, and now is, when the true worshipers will worship the Father in spirit and truth; for the Father is seeking such to worship Him" (Jo 4:23).

The call of Jesus in Scripture is not centered on our need, but on His presence. "Come unto me, all you who labor and are heavy laden, and I will give you rest" (Ma 11:28). He underscores this again in an account told by John, "On the last day, that great day of the feast, Jesus stood and cried out, saying, "If anyone thirsts, let him come to Me and drink" (Jo 7:37).

These calls invite us to come to Jesus. As we love and worship Him, our needs are met and necessary resources are released. The call of Jesus still rings across the centuries, "Come to Me." But this requires a discipline of time. Destiny comes to those who are not afraid to be alone with God!

The Glory of Service

In the Great Commission we are told that signs follow those who believe. "And these signs will follow those who believe; In My name they will cast out demons; they will speak with new tongues" (Mk 16:17). Too often, we are guilty of seeking signs instead of seeking Him. As we seek Christ by faith, everything else falls into place.

Furthermore, in evangelistic zeal, we often have answered the call to go before answering the summons to come! Our meager results give clear testimony to our powerlessness to penetrate our culture.

It is important for us to get the order right in ministry! Before Christ commissioned His disciples, they all sat at the common table with Jesus and soaked in His love and nurture. Before Pentecost, the disciples tarried, waiting to be clothed with power from on high. We are called to a relationship first, then we are ready for assignment!

I believe the church has fumbled away fifty percent of her members by pressing assignments upon people who have no intimate walk with Jesus Christ. In His greatest sermon, Jesus said, "But seek first the kingdom of God and His righteousness, and all these things shall be added to you" (Ma 6:33). We must come to our King to bow and worship *first,* and then He can add all the things we need to our lives.

Many great Bible figures found their ministry released only after a crisis during which they spent great amounts of time alone with God. (Moses, Elijah, David, Isaiah). It is the same for us today! Before we can reach others, there must be a solid relationship with Jesus. Before blessing must come breaking.

Alone with God

I've told already in this book about some of the pivotal "alone" times I've had with God. One of the most powerful occurred on a personal retreat several years ago. I had set aside four days and three nights with God, in a sparse and simply furnished cabin. As I drove up nearby Dayton Mountain, an expectancy filled my heart. I brought a CD player with worship music along with my computer with Bible programs on it and an unfinished book manuscript. I also brought a deep hunger and a serious need to know if I was moving with the Spirit. My spiritual awakening, including tongues, had become common knowledge in my circle of acquaintances, and there was unrest among many of our traditional church members.

Once settled in the cabin, I prayed, worshipped, wrote, and finally went to bed. In the wee hours of the morning, I was summoned to the stairs! My small room became a cathedral as God awakened me to join Him. He spoke and said, "It is time for you to act!" Looking at the clock by the bed, it was 3:19 a.m. I picked up my Bible and read Acts 3:19-21:

> Repent, then, and turn to God, so that your sins may be wiped out, that times of refreshing may come from the Lord, and that he may send the Christ, who has been appointed for you—even Jesus. He must remain in heaven until the time comes for God to restore everything, as he promised long ago through his holy prophets. (NIV)

I had a clear answer from God—He was up to something special in our church! He was refreshing us and drawing us into His presence. It was all God's doing and not mine. Then I reread that prophetic word, and it shook me. Jesus Christ would not return until a mighty restoration took place! God would restore to the church all that she had lost. A colossal revival was beginning in the body of Christ!

I immersed myself in the rest of the book of Acts, worshipping and feeding. Soon I came across Acts 15:16-17:

> After this I will return and rebuild David's fallen tent. Its ruins I will rebuild, and I will restore it, that the remnant of men may seek the Lord, and all the Gentiles who bear my name, says the Lord, who does these things. (NIV)

The passage shook me. I recalled how David's tabernacle was brought up with dancing and praise. It was a precursor to Solomon's Temple. Scripture was clear here—Jesus was coming, but not until the restoration of real praise and worship was established. As David walked, sang, danced, and ruled in God's presence, so will God's people do in the last days!

I walked out of that cabin far enough to get service to my cell phone and called my answering machine back in my office to pour the revelation word out. All that week, revelation continued to pour into my soul. Alone with God, my ministry direction was affirmed, strengthened, and challenged!

Moses—Meek and Mighty

One of the most powerful leaders in the Bible was Moses, liberator of Israel. He owed his greatness to the solitude that brought him into a face-to-face relationship with God. "So the Lord spoke to Moses face to face, as a man speaks to his friend" (Ex 33:11).

Between guiding a nation of over a million people and standing up to the powerful Egyptian pharaoh, how did Moses know what to do in his leadership position? He spent time in the secret place of God! He climbed the stairs to meet the Lord. Notice the following story from Scripture.

So the Lord said to Moses, "I will also do this thing that you have spoken; for you have found grace in My sight, and I know you by name." And he said, "Please, show me Your glory." Then He said, "I will make all My goodness pass before you, and I will proclaim the name of the LORD before you. I will be gracious to whom I will be gracious, and I will have compassion on whom I will have compassion." But He said, "You cannot see My face; for no man shall see Me, and live." And the LORD said, "Here is a place by Me, and you shall stand on the rock. So it shall be, while My glory passes by, that I will put you in the cleft of the rock, and will cover you with My hand while I pass by. Then I will take away My hand, and you shall see My back; but My face shall not be seen.

Exodus 33:17-23

Yahweh asked Moses what he desired, but Moses did not ask for anything for himself! His simple request was, "Show me Your glory." The response of Yahweh is thrilling and invites us to join Moses in his quest:

"Here is a place by Me . . . I will put you in the cleft of the rock, and will cover you with my hand while I pass by" (Ex 33:21-22).

Think of it! We can have a "place" by the Lord now, that "secret place" we've been longing for. God invites us to share in His glory. Oh, does your heart long to be close to Him? Do you desire an intimate relationship with Yahweh? We can have what Moses had and more if we desire Him with all of our heart. The NIV translates this phrase, "There is a place near Me." and the Living Bible states, ". . . Stand here on this rock beside Me . . ." What a powerful moment that must have been! Moses was so changed that even his face glowed with the glory of God! His nearness changes all who dare go with Him up the stairs to the cleft of the rock. Change and challenge flow from the mutual love shared in the secret place.

Moses' visit up the stairs determined the destiny of millions! Yahweh speaks to Moses in Exodus 34, sparing the people and giving them the ground rules for life.

Moses was forever changed! His face reflected the light of the Shekinah glory. He was so transformed that they had to put a veil over his face. Moses was marked by his visit with the Lord.

And when Moses had finished speaking with them, he put a veil on his face. But whenever Moses went in before the Lord to speak with Him, he would take the veil off until he came out; and he would come out and speak to the children of Israel whatever he had been commanded. And whenever the children of Israel saw the face of Moses, that the skin of Moses' face shone, then Moses would put the veil on his face again, until he went in to speak with Him.

Exodus 34:33-35

Later as the glory faded from Moses face, he still wore the veil in order to hide the fact that the glory was departing.

More than Moses

We can have more than Moses experienced! Thank God we do not have to live a moment without His glory. We can shine with His glory every day of our lives. Paul the apostle knew this, when he wrote,

Are we beginning to commend ourselves again? Or do we need, like some people, letters of recommendation to you or from you? You yourselves are our letter, written on our hearts, known and read by everybody. You show that you are a letter from Christ, the result of our ministry, written not with ink but with the Spirit of the living God, not on tablets of stone but on tablets of human hearts.

2 Corinthians 3:1-3 NIV

God has written upon our hearts by His Spirit a new law. This is the law of liberty! "He has made us competent as ministers of a new covenant—not of the letter but of the Spirit; for the letter kills, but the Spirit gives life" (2 Co 3:6 NIV).

Paul points out that when the law was given, it came with God's glory, and it was a minister of death. How much more glorious is what we have in the New Covenant! Lasting glory that doesn't fade away is ours!

Now if the ministry that brought death, which was engraved in letters on stone, came with glory, so that the Israelites could not look steadily at the face of Moses because of its glory, fading though it was, will not the ministry of the Spirit be even more glorious? If the ministry that condemns men is glorious, how much more glorious is the ministry that brings righteousness! For what was glorious has no glory now in comparison with the surpassing glory. And if what was fading away came with glory, how much greater is the glory of that which lasts!

2 Corinthians 3:7-11 NIV

Thank God we have an unfading glory. When you come to the Lord, the veil is removed and you may reflect the glory of the Lord Jesus.

Therefore, since we have such a hope, we are very bold. We are not like Moses, who would put a veil over his face to keep the Israelites from gazing at it while the radiance was fading away. But their minds were made dull, for to this day the same veil remains when the old covenant is read. It has not been removed, because only in

...n to this day when Moses is read, a veil
...enever anyone turns to the Lord, the veil
...ord is the Spirit, and where the Spirit of the
...om.

2 Corinthians 3:12-17 NIV

...ome truth makes us bold. We walk in freedom when the
...ord. His presence transforms us. As mentioned before, the glory
...in the Old Testament was indicated by the word *kabod*. From its
..., *kabod* meant "heavy." In its best sense, it meant to "be weighed down
with majesty and honor." Clearly, the kabod was visibly evident on the
person on whom it had been bestowed.

The New Testament word for glory was *doxa*, which means "praise,
honor, and dignity." This word comes from the obsolete root *deiknno*,
which literally meant "to show." Thus, it indicates that glory was visible on
those it touched. "But we all, with unveiled face, beholding as in a mirror
the glory of the Lord, are being transformed into the same image from
glory to glory, just as by the Spirit of the Lord" (2 Co 3:18).

Here is the clear promise of God. When we meet Him and ascend the
"stairs" into His presence, we reflect His glory. That glory that comes from
Jesus' presence transforms us.

The word "transformed" is the Greek *metamorphometha*. This word is
used only four times in all of the New Testament. In Matthew and Mark it
is used of the transfiguration of Jesus. "His face shone like the sun, and
His clothes became as white as the light" (Matthew 17:2). Here, the glory
of the Trinity shone through the human body of Jesus. This event was visible for all to see.

Paul used the word on two occasions.

I beseech you therefore, brethren, by the mercies of God, that you
present your bodies a living sacrifice, holy, acceptable to God, which
is your reasonable service. And do not be conformed to this world,
but be transformed by the renewing of your mind, that you may
prove what is that good and acceptable and perfect will of God.

Romans 12:1-2

Here the believer is called to total surrender in order that he
tally transformed. It calls to mind the incredible change that con
life cycle of a caterpillar, a creature that must die to self and freed
cased in a cocoon, only to emerge a glorious butterfly, who knows
as its limit.

Paul also used the term a second time in this passage: "But we all,
unveiled face, beholding as in a mirror the glory of the Lord, are be
transformed into the same image from glory to glory, just as by the Spir
of the Lord" (2 Co 3:18).

The changes that take place in any believer will be visible and obvious
to all who see them. The Spirit of the Lord will move us from glory to
glory all of our lives.

Changed from glory into glory,
Till in heav'n we take our place,
Till we cast our crowns before Thee,
Lost in wonder, love and praise.

—Charles Wesley, 1747

Having ascended the stairs and embraced its secret, you will never be
the same. Glory!

Chapter 10

Heart-Cry for the Holy

Watching television footage of multimillion-dollar homes sliding down hillsides in California recently, like most other people, I immediately thought, *What were those homeowners thinking? What logical person would purposely perch their house on the edge of a muddy and eroding hill and expect it to stay there?*

What's more amazing was to hear that many of those homeowners did not have house insurance to cover landslides, and so would seek government disaster relief funds so they could rebuild. And many would rebuild a few hundred feet from their original property—on my tax dollar!

Residing in such a precarious dwelling in a landslide zone or in areas where hurricanes are a threat, I would imagine that safety would become an all-encompassing concern for such homeowners. Living always in the shadow of impending disaster, the comforts of home would be continually tinged by worry.

Thankfully, the secret place of the Father is a haven of complete safety! "He who dwells in the secret place of the Most High shall abide under the shadow of the Almighty" (Ps 91:1). The night the Holy Spirit changed me forever, this was the Scripture that gave me clear direction into the presence of the Lord, and my heart found an abiding peace!

Charles Spurgeon said:

It is not every man who dwells there; no, not even every Christian man. There are some who come to God's house; but the man mentioned here dwells with the God of the house. There are some who worship in the outer court of the temple; but "He who dwells in the secret place of the Most High" (Ps 91:1) lives in the Holy of Holies; he draws near to the mercy seat, and keeps there; he walks in the light, as God is in the light; he is not one who is sometimes on and sometimes off, a stranger or a guest, but like a child at home, he dwells in the secret place of the most High. Oh, labour to get to that blessed position! You who know the Lord, pray that you may attain to this high condition of dwelling in the inner shrine, always near to God, always overshadowed by those cherubic wings which indicate the presence of God. If this is your position, you "shall abide under the shadow of the Almighty." You are not safe in the outer courts; you are not protected from all danger anywhere but within the veil. Let us come boldly there; and, when we once enter, let us dwell there.[*]

It is by God's favor and grace and not our works that we enter this secret place with God. Of course it is not our work, but His work in us that draws us to the stairs.

The Hope of Glory

This is the potential dwelling place of all who are saved and know that Christ indwells them. "To them God willed to make known what are the riches of the glory of this mystery among the Gentiles; which is Christ in you, the hope of glory" (Col 1:27).

The divine mystery Paul speaks of is the believer dwelling *now* in the Holy of Holies, the very presence of God. Because Jesus abides in you, you are tied by hope to His throne. The word *hope* is from the Greek *elpis* meaning "anchor rope." The anchor rope of hope tugs your heart heavenward! There is a powerful pulling in all of us toward this destiny. The goal of the Christian life is that all of us would find ourselves "complete" in Christ. Look again at Colossians 1:29: "To this end I also labor, striving according to His working which works in me mightily."

Here the great apostle is referring to his work as if he was in labor pain for birth, as if he is in agony, and the very energy of heaven is moving him to supernatural power. The place of God's glory, where He is worshipped, is the place of His mighty power.

---

[*] from *Spurgeon's Sermons,* an electronic database © 1997, Biblesoft

You see, it is possible for you to dwell, to really establish your life in the place of God's glory!

The One Condition

Again I ask, how do I get to this secret place? Must I wrestle as Jacob? Must I run as Elijah? Must I weep as Isaiah? Must I be martyred as Paul? No, these are only the outward circumstances that lead us to the simple secret of His presence. The answer lies in having a depth of spiritual hunger and thirst. God is looking for some people with a desire as strong as a parched and thirsty man lost in a desert. Such a man would give all he owned in a desperate moment for a lifesaving drink of water.

Our desperate cry for Him should be wholehearted and passionate! In Scripture, we find out how to seek Him, and discover promises from the Father for those who are thirsty.

Are you . . .

LIKE A DEER RUNNING FROM A HUNTER?
As the deer pants for the water brooks,
> So pants my soul for You, O God.
My soul thirsts for God, for the living God.
> When shall I come and appear before God? (Ps 42:1-2)

LIKE A WEARY WORSHIPPER TIRED OF THE ORDINARY?
O God, You are my God;
> Early will I seek You;
> My soul thirsts for You;
> My flesh longs for You
> In a dry and thirsty land
> Where there is no water.
So I have looked for You in the sanctuary,
> To see Your power and Your glory.
Because Your lovingkindness is better than life,
> My lips shall praise You.
Thus I will bless You while I live;
> I will lift up my hands in Your name. (Ps 63:1-4)

LIKE A TIRED TRAVELER ON A JOURNEY?
Hungry and thirsty,
> Their soul fainted in them.
Then they cried out to the LORD in their trouble,
> And He delivered them out of their distresses. (Ps 107:5-6)

Then act!

STRETCH YOUR HANDS TOWARD HIM!
> I spread out my hands to You; My soul longs for You like a thirsty land. (Ps 143:6)

CLAIM HIS PROMISE OF OUTPOURED BLESSING!
For I will pour water on him who is thirsty,
And floods on the dry ground;
I will pour My Spirit on your descendants,
And My blessing on your offspring. (Is 44:3)

RESPOND AND COME BEFORE HIS GRACE!
Ho! Everyone who thirsts,
> Come to the waters;
> And you who have no money,
> Come, buy and eat.
> Yes, come, buy wine and milk
> Without money and without price. (Is 55:1)

REALIZE YOU ARE INVITED NOT TO RELIGION, BUT TO JESUS.
On the last day, that great day of the feast, Jesus stood and cried out, saying, "If anyone thirsts, let him come to Me and drink." (Jo 7:37)

YOUR RESPONSIBILITY IS TO COME.
And He said to me, "It is done! I am the Alpha and the Omega, the Beginning and the End. I will give of the fountain of the water of life freely to him who thirsts." (Re 21:6)

WHEN YOU ARRIVE, YOU MAY DRINK OF HIM.
And the Spirit and the bride say, "Come!" And let him who hears say, "Come!" And let him who thirsts come. Whoever desires, let him take the water of life freely. (Re 22:17)

In Matthew 5:6, Jesus says, "Blessed are those who hunger and thirst for righteousness, For they shall be filled." My only requirement is a holy dissatisfaction with all that is around me. My heart must be thirsty for Jesus and Him alone. I can hear Him calling me up the stairs into the High Place where there flows an artesian well of life. It is mine to enjoy. I may drink or I may splash in it like a child on a hot summer day. I come, oh Lord! Indeed, I come with all my heart and soul!

Step onto the Stairs!

If thirst is the condition then faith is the motivation. Faith must take the step up and into the secret place of the most high. Psalm 91 tells us to come into this place, and to plan to stay! When you dwell somewhere, you sit down, settle in, inhabit, as if you were firmly established in housekeeping as a married couple would be. It is the word used in Psalm 23:6: "I will dwell in the house of the Lord forever." A decision to enter is irreversible. This is a "forever" commitment.

In the award-winning movie, *The Matrix,* reality has been clothed by an invisible force. All of humanity is enslaved and has become sources of energy for a world run by evil machines. Humans are basically living out a false life that is no more than a dream. A few humans manage to break through to reality and find their former world in shambles. Those who broke through discovered they couldn't go back to their old lives and must become soldiers dedicated to the task of saving the rest of enslaved humanity.

Our world has a matrix of evil and deception. Once we have broken through to the spiritual world, we will never be satisfied to go back to our former reality of a life void of intimacy with God.

In coming to God, we also must recognize His sovereignty. He is Most High God, El Elyon. There must be no rival in our hearts to Him. He is El Shaddai, God Almighty. *Shaddai* literally refers to "the breasted One," the

One who nurtures and cares for you as a mother would for her child. He alone can fill our spiritual thirst and satisfy our hungry soul.

Finally, I must confess my faith and trust in Him to enter. He is "my refuge," "my fortress," and "My God, in Him will I trust" (Ps 91:2).

Faith bids us to step into His presence. This is my final and irrevocable choice, to live in the secret place of the stairs.

Chapter 11

Abiding in the Almighty

In biblical times and even today, devout Jewish men worshipping in the temple wore a covering called a *talith* or prayer cloth. This shielding was a symbol that they were spending intimate time alone with God.

That is what our secret place is like—a covering. King David wrote, "He who dwells in the secret place of the Most High Shall abide under the shadow of the Almighty" (Ps 91:1). We are to "abide" under the shadow of the Almighty. The word *abide* means "to tarry all night." It speaks of the intimacy of lovers, husband and wife, who tarry all night loving each other. Here is the divine glory covering us, loving us, and hovering protectively over us.

Having entered this close relationship with Jesus by trust, we become the beneficiaries of divine favor!

A Place of Protection

Like a young eagle in its mother's nest, you are safe on the stairs. His truth covers and protects you.

He shall cover you with His feathers,
And under His wings you shall take refuge;
His truth shall be your shield and buckler.
You shall not be afraid of the terror by night,
Nor of the arrow that flies by day.

Ps 91:4-5

Night terrors are a great problem with many today, children and adults alike. Fears of the dark remain with some youngsters into their adult lives. Yet the unknown night stalkers of hell have no right or place on the stairs! No arrow of the wicked can penetrate the shield of faith and trust that guards the entrance to the secret place! In His presence, the old fears leave. God promises, "A thousand may fall at your side, And ten thousand at your right hand; But it shall not come near you" (Ps 91:7). While others may become victims of the enemy, you will be safe because of your close relationship to Him.

Some years ago, a demented man approached me after a revival service in another city. He was about to hit me in the parking lot when Eddie Adams, my staff assistant, grabbed the man's arm. With his other hand, Eddie pushed me into the car and faced my attacker for me. That night, Eddie was literally my shield!

If we abide in this place of protection, then we have Jesus and his angelic hosts present to step in for us.

> For He shall give His angels charge over you,
>   To keep you in all your ways.
> In their hands they shall bear you up,
>   Lest you dash your foot against a stone.
>
>   Psalm 91:11-12

Avoiding Evil

"No evil shall befall you, nor shall any plague come near your dwelling" (Ps 91:10).

There is just something about the name, *Jesus*! His name is power, and within the folds of its protection, believers can know a secret place where there is anointing, safety, and blessing—a tower of strength that keeps us from evil! Our planet has become "the killing fields" of hell, yet we can live immune to all these plagues.

Here is a place where neither devil nor disease can disturb our walk or destroy our witness for Jesus. You see, we go in His strength! We actually carry His dwelling with us! Angels watch over our every step. "Are they not all ministering spirits sent forth to minister for those who will inherit salvation?" (He 1:14).

How can you find that place of safety? Look at these four keys to avoid-ing evil found in Psalm 91.

Intimacy

If you are going to avoid evil, you must have an intimate relationship with Jesus Christ. In just the first two verses of Psalm 91, we find four different names of God! Our Maker wants us to know His name, to know His very character.

How do you get into God's presence and abide there? Here is the golden gateway into God's presence: "I will say of the Lord, 'He is my refuge and my fortress; my God, in Him I will trust'" (Ps 91:2). You see, God inhabits praise! When we begin to audibly confess His Word out of our mouth, when we extol His might and power, then we discover the place of intimacy with Him! You move into what the psalmist David called the secret place of the Most High, an open door to His presence.

Invincibility

Once you've come to a place of intimacy, you move on to a place of invincibility. In the safety of the shadow of His presence, Psalm 91 tells us we will escape many traps of the enemy, that God will "deliver you from the snare of the fowler." In biblical times, a snare was what was used to catch birds or animals, containing a lure or bait. The devil sets dangerous traps for believers, but those who are walking and talking and speaking forth who Jesus is will be delivered from these traps, including deception, doubt, darkness, demonic forces, disease, disasters, and defeat.

If you are hearing from God and walking with Him on a daily basis, it doesn't mean that disasters won't happen. It doesn't mean the disease doesn't come. It simply means that those things cannot stop you.

Immunity

There is a difference between invincibility and immunity. Invincibility means you can escape evil's trap. Immunity means that long before it gets to your borders, you'll know and you will be out of the way.

Millions of dollars have been spent placing tsunami-warning systems into the Indian Ocean following the devastation that hit in December 2004. These new devices are ultra-sensitive, sending a split-second signal to a satellite if the ocean rises even a foot, and warning affected countries within moments of detection. This reminds us of the power of our connection with God, for His warning system gives us notice and prompting long before evil can come to hinder our path!

In the historic home of John Wesley, the great Methodist, there is a very small upstairs room. This was his prayer room which he used daily at 4:30 a.m. No wonder so many hymns, so much ministry, and so much anointing flowed out of Wesley. He had an appointment with God at 4:30 each morning! As a result, this promise was his: "Because you have made the Lord, who is my refuge, Even the Most High, your dwelling place, No evil shall befall you, Nor shall any plague come near your dwelling" (Ps 91:9-10).

Increase

What's the final secret to avoiding evil? When we go after God as an ardent lover, when we pursue Him with passion (Ps 91:14), God promises to give seven things to us:

Spiritual victory— "I will deliver him"
Spiritual influence— "I will set him on high"
Spiritual access to God—"I will answer him"
Spiritual protection—"I will be with him in trouble"
Spiritual favor—"I will honor him"
Spiritual fullness—"I will satisfy him"
Spiritual insight—"I will show him My salvation."

The condition of our protection is that we dwell in God. When He is our "address" then the devil cannot approach.

His promise is to "set you on high" because you "set your love on Him." To be set on high indicates honor, to be made excellent, to be shown and proclaimed as special! God has made you significant and special because you love Him.

Richard Roberts, Oral Roberts' son, once explained the circumstances surrounding the beginnings of Oral Roberts University. "Ron, I want to tell you how dad approached the project," he said. "We almost went under here because we got to depending on fund-raisers and depending on this and depending on that. But then dad began walking out onto the property, before we even owned it, taking an open Bible with him. He would read Scripture and pray in the Spirit, because he had had a vision from God."

Can you hear the heart of God? You don't have to live alone. He is the God of the universe and He loves you. He's looking for some people who will set their love on Him, who will know His name, who will pursue Him, who will keep their appointment with Him, who will know Him. You need Jesus. You need His power and His presence in your life. The God of creation will meet you right in the middle of your need!

What's in a Name?

In the Old Testament, a person's name was more than simply a tag. Rather, it represented the character, virtue, family essence, and resources of an individual. When we whisper the name "Jesus," we are uttering the mightiest, most majestic Name of all time, the magnum opus of all titles given to the Almighty!

David Kaplan was a Chicago sports personality who decided his name was worth more than riches! Dallas Maverick's owner, Mark Cuban, asked the sportscaster to consider changing his name to "Dallas Maverick"! Cuban even offered $50,000 to Kaplan if he would do it! Kaplan balked, and so Cuban upped the offer to $100,000, plus another $100,000 to go to Kaplan's favorite charity, and said that Kaplan would only have to adopt the name change for one year!

What would you do?

Kaplan decided to decline the generous offer. A *Chicago Tribune* article quoted him explaining, "My name is my birthright. I'd like to preserve my integrity and credibility."

Our loving God established His name in the earth, a Name above all Names! As we approach the secret place, what a joy it is to speak the name of Jesus, and experience the wonder of the mighty character of the Lord!

In Matthew 16, Jesus laid the foundational truth upon which He would assemble His people into the body and family we call the church. It is interesting that Jesus began this lesson to His own insiders by asking them to tell Him his name. "He said to them, 'But who do you say that I am?' " (Ma 16:15).

This is the essential question of the Christian life, the only question on the final exam of Christian possibility! If we do not know His name, we will not be able to abide in Him and do His work. After spending three years with His disciples, Jesus wanted to know their perception of Him. Peter got an A+ for his answer:

> Simon Peter answered and said, "You are the Christ, the Son of the living God." Jesus answered and said to him, "Blessed are you, Simon Bar-Jonah, for flesh and blood has not revealed this to you, but My Father who is in heaven. And I also say to you that you are Peter, and on this rock I will build My church, and the gates of Hades shall not prevail against it."
>
> Matthew 16:16-18

Peter knew Jesus' name the same way we can know it—by Divine revelation. The Holy Spirit revealed that in Jesus dwelt the fullness of God. It is in knowing the revelation of His name that God would build His church. God is building up people who know who Christ is and want to worship and spend time with Him.

Numbers or People?

God is not interested in our "facts and figures" or about how many people pass in and out of our church doors. He is not seeking statistics, but worshippers.

> But the hour is coming, and now is, when the true worshipers will worship the Father in spirit and truth; for the Father is seeking such to worship Him. God is Spirit, and those who worship Him must worship in spirit and truth.
>
> John 4:23-24

We win souls in order that those people will give glory and honor to the Lord Jesus Christ. This militant worshipping body that knows no name but His will take down the gates of hell and death. Knowing His name is to know His anointing that breaks every yoke. He is Messiah, the anointed One who alone reigns over all. Hell must swing open its prison house before the anointed, singing Bride.

The Keys to Everything

When we get inside the secret place, the name of Jesus releases the keys to the kingdom. Everything we need is now available. He has given us the means to unlock every resource needed to finish the work He has called us to do. From shortage to abundance, from weakness to strength, and from defeat to victory! All of these blessings flow to us in His presence. Note these keys promised to us:

Key of David—Praise and Worship (Re 3:7)
Key of the House of David—Kingdom resources (Is 22:22)
Keys of Death and Hell—the Good News of Jesus (Re 1:18).

Everything flows to those who know His name! "I will give you the keys of the kingdom of heaven; and whatever you bind on earth shall have been bound in heaven, and whatever you loose on earth shall have been loosed in heaven" (Ma 16:19 NASB).

What an exciting promise, to know that we will see what God is doing in heaven and declare it bound or loosed on earth! Our prayers, instead of hit or miss, become informed. In His presence, we discover what He is saying and doing, and by the prayer of faith, move it to earth.

Psalm 91:14-16 reveals more clear promises to those who dwell in His presence, love His Name, and have no desire but to know Him better.

I will deliver him . . .
    This means the enemy will never hold you in sin's spiritual prison!

I will set him on high . . .

God will take care of your reputation. Let promotion come from the Lord.

He shall call upon Me, and I will answer . . .

God will always answer your prayers.

I will be with him in trouble . . .

This promise assures me I never will face anything alone! In Matthew 28:20, Jesus said: "Lo, I am with you always, even to the end of the age."

I will honor him . . .

Only the applause of heaven really matters. His "well done" is enough.

With long life I will satisfy him . . .

God will extend our days so that we will live a satisfied, full, and overflowing life and will leave this life with blazing energy across the finish line!

I will show him My salvation.

The word for salvation in this passage is *Yeshua* which is Hebrew for Jesus! Thus, the best promise is saved for last—God will show us Jesus! To see Jesus is the beginning and end of everything.

Something About that Name

There is such significance in knowing God's name. This "knowing" means much more than head knowledge; rather, it refers to the closest possible intimacy, as a man knows his wife. To know God's name is to be an intimate who has learned all the facets and nuances of His character. The name of Jesus encompasses so much! He is:

Yahweh—the Great I Am
Jireh—my Provider
Tsidkenu—my Righteousness
Rophe—my Healer
Rohi—my Shepherd

Nissi—my Leader and Lover
Shalom—my Peace
Shammah—my Companion

Yes, He is also our Christ, the Anointed One, and the Messiah of the world. He is Wonderful! He is our Lord! He is before the beginning and after the end! He is the unceasing song of David resounding across time and all of creation! He is the Ever Shining Star that shall never fade.

Christ Jesus is the One who we meet on the stairs. It is His scarred hand that takes us up, and His shining face that welcomes us in. On the stairs, we will whisper His name, Jesus, and find ourselves abiding in the Almighty, overwhelmed with the promise and blessing of His presence!

Chapter 12

Our Man Upstairs

The only way we could ever get to that secret place of the stairs is for someone to draw us there. An invitation, a pulling, a drawing . . . in every instance, when someone has made the journey, Christ Himself has escorted them.

Consider . . . who wrestled all night with Jacob? Who spoke from a burning bush? Whom did Isaiah see in the Holy of Holies? Who blinded Saul of Tarsus on the roadside? Who danced with David? Who came to Abraham's tent and declared words of hope? It was Jesus Christ! He lived and operated long before His incarnation as a babe in Bethlehem. Ultimately He had to come and make a way for us all.

Out of the Ivory Palaces

The kingdom of God must break through to the earth. In order for that to happen, the King must come in person. David often sang of the promise of God, that an anointed King would come out of the ivory palaces to be our hiding place:

Your throne, O God, is forever and ever;
> A scepter of righteousness is the scepter of Your kingdom.
You love righteousness and hate wickedness;
> Therefore God, Your God, has anointed You
> With the oil of gladness more than Your companions.
All Your garments are scented with myrrh and aloes and cassia,
> Out of the ivory palaces, by which they have made You glad.

Psalm 45:6-8

David had always known that this coming One was his refuge and safety. He wrote, "You are my hiding place; You shall preserve me from trouble; You shall surround me with songs of deliverance." (Ps 32:7)

The Coming One inhabited David's praise, surrounding him with songs of deliverance! A more recent hymn writer echoed David's joy:

Wonderful, wonderful Jesus
In the heart He implanteth a song;
A song of deliverance, of courage, of strength,
In the heart He implanteth a song.

—Anna B. Russell, 1921

In addition, the Coming One protected David through the Word. Jesus shows up when His Word is rightly received and released. We can say with David, "You are my hiding place and my shield; I hope in Your word" (Ps 119:114).

Rock of All the Ages

The promise of a Man who would come as a hiding place fills the Old Testament. The prophet Isaiah possibly saw more of Jesus in revelation than any other prophet. Isaiah met Jesus on the secret place of the stairs and saw much of the life of Jesus 700 years early! Look at this powerful passage: "A man will be as a hiding place from the wind, And a cover from the tempest, As rivers of water in a dry place, As the shadow of a great rock in a weary land" (Is 32:2).

Here it clearly states that "a Man" would be the secret place, the hiding place. No wind, no storm, and no flood can find the child of God who has fled to the Man on the stairs.

The Lord Jesus Christ came to earth in order that we might go up! His descent from that world beyond is outstanding and miraculous. Oh, how powerful was that love that paved a way to the Father!

Oh, the love that drew salvation's plan!
Oh, the grace that brought it down to man!

Oh, the mighty gulf that God did span
At Calvary.

—William Newell

What an awesome descent! Look at its record in Scripture:

Let this mind be in you which was also in Christ Jesus, who, being in
the form of God, did not consider it robbery to be equal with God, but
made Himself of no reputation, taking the form of a bondservant, and
coming in the likeness of men. And being found in appearance as a
man, He humbled Himself and became obedient to the point of death,
even the death of the cross. Therefore God also has highly exalted Him
and given Him the name which is above every name, that at the name
of Jesus every knee should bow, of those in heaven, and of those on
earth, and of those under the earth, and that every tongue should confess that Jesus Christ is Lord, to the glory of God the Father.

Philippians 2:5-11

God laid aside His rights as God. God came down, became a human
being, essentially assuming the position of slave. The journey continues as
the Perfect One dies. This death was another step down the stairs toward
us, for He died on a cross, the place of the curse. Oh, the horror of it for
Him, but the joy of that sacrifice for us! He came down to pay our way out
and to invite us to climb the stairs back up to that place where "every knee
shall bow and every tongue should confess that Jesus Christ is Lord, to the
glory of God the Father" (Ph 2:10-11).

Down from His glory, ever living story
Our God as Savior came, and Jesus was His name.
Born in a manger, to the world a stranger;
A Man of Sorrows, tears, and agony.
Oh, how I love Him! How I adore Him!
My breath, my sunshine! My all in all!
The Great Creator became my Savior,
And all God's fullness dwelleth in Him.

—William E. Booth

Jesus Sought the Stairs

One of the most touching passages in the gospel is found in John 17. This chapter records a tender prayer that Jesus prayed for His followers, both those from that time and ours as well. His intercession for us revealed His desire for His people to know the Father intimately. Jesus' words are a direct reflection of His heart.

It is significant to note that Jesus longed for the stairs Himself while He was here on earth! "I have glorified You on the earth. I have finished the work which You have given Me to do. And now, O Father, glorify Me together with Yourself, with the glory which I had with You before the world was" (Jo 17:4-5).

The Intimacy of His Name

Our Lord came to manifest the *name* of God to us. Here again we see the importance of God's name. To know His name is to be intimate with Him. Jesus prayed to His Father, "I have manifested Your name to the men whom You have given Me out of the world. They were Yours, You gave them to Me, and they have kept Your word" (Jo 17:6).

The apostle Paul elevated the name of Jesus to the highest possible place:

Therefore God also has highly exalted Him and given Him the name which is above every name, that at the name of Jesus every knee should bow, of those in heaven, and of those on earth, and of those under the earth, and that every tongue should confess that Jesus Christ is Lord, to the glory of God the Father.

Philippians 2:9-11

Salt and Light

Looking further into the prayer of Jesus in John 17, we hear His heartbeat and desire. Jesus does not want to take us out of the world, but desires that we should live lives that penetrate the world with God's truth. We are to be kept, sanctified, Word-centered, and mission-oriented:

I do not pray that You should take them out of the world, but that You should keep them from the evil one. They are not of the world, just as I am not of the world. Sanctify them by Your truth. Your word is truth. As You sent Me into the world, I also have sent them into the world. And for their sakes I sanctify Myself, that they also may be sanctified by the truth.

John 17:15-19

In the ancient baptismal rituals of the church, the candidate would begin by renouncing Satan and then confessing Jesus as Lord. Then the elder would place a bit of salt on the new Christian's tongue, saying, "You are the salt of the earth . . ." Later, the candidate would be given a lighted candle, and would be charged, "You are the light of the world . . ." The elders wanted to impress upon the new believer that, having drawn near to Jesus, he would share the same heartbeat to help a decaying and dark world.

Jesus' heartfelt prayer reaches all the way to where we are today. Jesus prays for unity among fellow believers, so that God may manifest His glorious presence, and so that the lost may clearly see Him.

I do not pray for these alone, but also for those who will believe in Me through their word; that they all may be one, as You, Father, are in Me, and I in You; that they also may be one in Us, that the world may believe that You sent Me. And the glory which You gave Me I have given them, that they may be one just as We are one: I in them, and You in Me; that they may be made perfect in one, and that the world may know that You have sent Me, and have loved them as You have loved Me.

John 17:20-23

How can a people move to this position of unity, power, and glory? We must learn that an intimate relationship with Jesus is more important than religion's trappings and labels. Listen to the end of this prayer, for Jesus earnestly prays that we might know the intimacy with the Father that He knows:

Father, I desire that they also whom You gave Me may be with Me where I am, that they may behold My glory which You have given

Me; for You loved Me before the foundation of the world. O right-eous Father! The world has not known You, but I have known You; and these have known that You sent Me. And I have declared to them Your name, and will declare it, that the love with which You loved Me may be in them, and I in them.

John 17:24-26

Wow! I can experience the same "glory" with the Father that Jesus experienced! God's goal for my life and Jesus' prayer for my life is that I might get into His presence and experience His love and power. That is why He came and why He died. He is our Rock of all the ages. May our prayer be that of David:

Hear my cry, O God; Attend to my prayer. From the end of the earth I will cry to You, When my heart is overwhelmed; Lead me to the rock that is higher than I. For You have been a shelter for me, A strong tower from the enemy. I will abide in Your tabernacle forever; I will trust in the shelter of Your wings.

Psalm 61:1-4

Oh, thank God for the Rock that is higher than I!

Rock of Ages, cleft for me,
Let me hide myself in Thee;
Let the water and the blood,
From thy wounded side which flowed,
Be of sin, the double cure,
Save from wrath and make me pure.

—Augustus Toplady

THE UPWARD CHALLENGE

Chapter 13

The Doorway
of Discipline

The rewards for a praying Christian are great. Unimaginable blessings can be released through fervent prayer. Martin Luther said, "Prayer is not overcoming God's reluctance, but laying hold of His willingness."

Our Lord Jesus Christ modeled and underscored the value of the secret of the stairs. During His entire three-year public ministry, we read of many times He personally withdrew, even from His inner circle, to be alone with His Father. I am totally convinced that Jesus' unbroken communion with the Father made His ministry powerfully effective.

Jesus acted out on earth what He saw the Father doing in heaven. He was fully man, so He too had to get to the secret place of the stairs to know the Father's plan. Read this remarkable report of Jesus:

> Then Jesus answered and said to them, "Most assuredly, I say to you, the Son can do nothing of Himself, but what He sees the Father do; for whatever He does, the Son also does in like manner. For the Father loves the Son, and shows Him all things that He Himself does; and He will show Him greater works than these, that you may marvel."

John 5:19-20

Because of the love relationship between the Father and Son, the Son had inside information on everything the Father was doing. More astounding than this is the glorious inclusion of you and I in the inner circle of the Trinity! God desires to reveal to us what He is doing, that our lives might be adjusted to His purposes.

More Than Head Knowledge

The most religiously zealous characters of New Testament times missed the opportunity of true intimacy with God. These were Biblical scholars who knew the Old Testament in its original language. They were closely familiar with every letter of the greatest commentaries of their day. They could sit at the feet of the greatest rabbis. Yet, they missed the point! Bible study is worthless if it does not bring you into an audience with its author and teacher.

> "You search the Scriptures, for in them you think you have eternal life; and these are they which testify of Me. But you are not willing to come to Me that you may have life."
>
> John 5:39-40

You can know the Bible and miss a relationship with Jesus! But the Scriptures, when unlocked by the revelation of the Spirit of God, show us what it is that pleases the Father.

The Heavenly Comforter

Jesus released His freedom, giving truth to people who lived in His word. Everywhere He went, He spread that freedom, telling all, "And you shall know the truth, and the truth shall make you free" (Jo 8:32).

To some, it was the first taste of truth they had ever known. The woman at the well received "living water" to replace the stale sordid state of her life. Jesus assured her, "whoever drinks of the water that I shall give him will never thirst. But the water that I shall give him will become in him a fountain of water springing up into everlasting life" (Jo 4:14).

To others, He gave a call to return to the freedoms that they knew were available from Jehovah. Jesus invited the nation to quit worshipping the past and instead determine to move into a fresh experience with Him.

As the mighty and eternal Rock, He still gives forth the water of life to this day! This water becomes a mighty river of ministry, as He so boldly declared in the book of John.

> On the last day, that great day of the feast, Jesus stood and cried out, saying, "If anyone thirsts, let him come to Me and drink. He who believes in Me, as the Scripture has said, out of his heart will flow rivers of living water." But this He spoke concerning the Spirit, whom those believing in Him would receive; for the Holy Spirit was not yet given, because Jesus was not yet glorified.
>
> John 7:37-39

In John 14, 15, and 16, Jesus releases the promise of the Holy Spirit. In your own study of these passages, look for the blessings that surround the ministry of the Spirit!

The Holy Spirit is Our Comforter—(14:16)
The Holy Spirit is Our Companion—(14:16-17)
The Holy Spirit is Our Teacher—(14:26, 15:26, and 16:17)
The Holy Spirit will Show Us Things to Come—(16:12-13)

Lessons on the Stairs

In Jesus' most well-known sermon, He taught the key spiritual disciplines. In Matthew 6, we find these three points of encouragement that vault us to the stairs.

Jesus Cares for the Poor

Charitable deeds or alms are acts that help the poor and needy. When you reach out to others at His prompting, do not announce it, just do it! Sow the seed when God shows the need.

Listen to His promise! God reveals this to us on the stairs,

Take heed that you do not do your charitable deeds before men, to be seen by them. Otherwise you have no reward from your Father in heaven. Therefore, when you do a charitable deed, do not sound a trumpet before you as the hypocrites do in the synagogues and in the streets, that they may have glory from men. Assuredly, I say to you, they have their reward. But when you do a charitable deed, do not let your left hand know what your right hand is doing, that your charitable deed may be in secret; and your Father who sees in secret will Himself reward you openly. And when you pray, you shall not be like the hypocrites. For they love to pray standing in the synagogues and on the corners of the streets, that they may be seen by men. Assuredly, I say to you, they have their reward. But you, when you pray, go into your room, and when you have shut your door, pray to your Father who is in the secret place; and your Father who sees in secret will reward you openly.

And when you pray, do not use vain repetitions as the heathen do. For they think that they will be heard for their many words.

Therefore do not be like them. For your Father knows the things you have need of before you ask Him. In this manner, therefore, pray:

Our Father in heaven,
Hallowed be Your name.
Your kingdom come.
Your will be done
On earth as it is in heaven.
Give us this day our daily bread.
And forgive us our debts,
As we forgive our debtors.
And do not lead us into temptation,
But deliver us from the evil one.
For Yours is the kingdom and the power and the glory forever.
Amen.

For if you forgive men their trespasses, your heavenly Father will also forgive you.

Matthew 6:1-14

Our social conscience is best stirred and guided by our devotional experience with God. There are more needs in those we see around us than we could ever hope to try and meet. How can we know who to help? How can we know clearly our mission? Only in "the secret place" can the Father instruct us.

Jesus Loves Prayer

Our best praying will be done when we are alone with God. It pleases God for us to talk to Him. More often than not, prayers are offered to whatever audience may be around. But prayer is meant to be our personal communication with God, not a flowery show for others.

If the early church had primarily confined their prayer language to the secret place, it is doubtful the church would have suffered division over it. Public prayer is almost nonexistent in Scripture, but private devotional time is discussed again and again. Our prayerlessness is the greatest sin of the church. When we closet ourselves away with God, He speaks clearly and powerfully. It pleases God for us to pray.

It is a fact that prayer can affect national destiny! The United States weathered many storms over the years due to the fervent intercession of leaders and saints. Consider this Proclamation issued by President Abraham Lincoln in 1863:

Whereas, the Senate of the United States, devoutly recognizing the Supreme Authority and just Government of the Almighty God in all the affairs of men and of nations, has, by a resolution, requested the President to designate and set apart a day for national prayer and humiliation.

And whereas it is the duty of nations as well as of men, to own their dependence upon the overruling power of God, to confess their sins and transgressions, in humble sorrow, yet with assured hope that genuine repentance will lead to mercy and pardon; and to recognize the sublime truth, announced in the Holy Scriptures and proven by all history, that those nations only are blessed whose God is the Lord. . . .

We have been the recipients of the choicest bounties of Heaven . . . We have grown in numbers, wealth and power as no other nation . . . But we have forgotten God . . . and we have vainly imagined, in the deceitfulness of our hearts, that all these blessings were produced by some superior wisdom and virtue of our own. Intoxicated with unbroken success, we have become too self-sufficient to feel the necessity of redeeming and preserving grace, too proud to pray to the God that made us!

It behooves us then, to humble ourselves before the offended Power, to confess our national sins and to pray for clemency and forgiveness.

Now . . . I do . . . designate and set apart Thursday, the 30th day of April, 1863, as a day of national humiliation, fasting and prayer. And I do hereby request all the people to abstain, on that day, from their ordinary secular pursuits, and to unite, at their several places of public worship and their respective homes, in keeping the day holy to the Lord . . .

Let us then rest humbly in the hope . . . that the united cry of the Nation will be heard on high, and answered with blessings, no less than the pardon of our national sins, and the restoration of our now divided and suffering Country, to its former happy condition of unity and peace.

In witness whereof, I have hereunto set my hand and caused the seal of the United States to be affixed.

—Abraham Lincoln

There is no doubt this bold statement by a godly president impacted our nation. How we need that spirit of humility and prayer once again!

Specifics of Prayer

The time we set aside to commune with God should be cleared of any other interests or activities. The instruction is clear: "But you, when you pray, go into your room, and when you have shut your door, pray to your Father who is in the secret place; and your Father who sees in secret will reward you openly" (Ma. 6:6). Not even food should be a distraction to the season we set aside to be alone with God. Our passion and hunger for Him drives away all other passions. The power of faith is seen in its privacy.

Our Father sees us in secret, yet rewards us publicly. Too often we do service in order to receive outward accolades, missing our true rewards. If we keep council with our Lord, He will reward us in due season.

If you are to stay in His presence, you can bring no grudge. If you are to gain an audience with the crucified One, let the scars He bore for you drive out your unforgiving spirit. Jesus instructed us, "If you forgive men their trespasses, your heavenly Father will also forgive you. But if you do not forgive men their trespasses, neither will your Father forgive your trespasses" (Ma 6:14-15).

It is doubtful you can climb the stairs and know God's secrets with an unforgiving attitude. In fact, you may be carrying this attitude as a witness that you are lost and your soul is in peril.

Kingdom Values

On the stairs, God wrestles us out of our materialism. The idol of "things" must be cast down. Our toys matter little in the light of His presence. He teaches us to invest now in the only place and time we will ever have opportunity to give to Him.

Do not lay up for yourselves treasures on earth, where moth and rust destroy and where thieves break in and steal; but lay up for yourselves treasures in heaven, where neither moth nor rust destroys and where thieves do not break in and steal.

Matthew 6:19-20

New Priorities

Jesus commands me to make Him the number one focus of my life. "But seek first the kingdom of God and His righteousness, and all these things shall be added to you" (Ma 6:33). My seeking involves longing for Jesus to be King over my life and over all the earth. This is the centerpiece of all spiritual growth and promise. I seek Him who has sought me and loved me from all eternity. Time, money, family, and future will all fall into place when you embrace Jesus as Lord over everything in your heart and life!

Chapter 14

School of the Spirit

What could change a small Jewish man with bad eyes and a hatred for Jesus Christ and make Him a passionate follower of the one he used to hate? The answer? A supernatural, unquestionable dose of God's grace, combined with a sure passing of time.

The apostle Paul's early ministry was a total disaster. Being a Jew, he assumed his ministry would be to the Jews. He was wrong, for his very presence seemed to only wreak havoc for the church. It became so bad at times that Paul finally had to be rescued from the city of Damascus, escaping over a wall in a basket lowered by a handful of the more tolerant believers!

Seminary of the Stairs

Paul said, "I will not boast about myself, except about my weaknesses. Even if I should choose to boast, I would not be a fool, because I would be speaking the truth. But I refrain, so no one will think more of me than is warranted by what I do or say" (2 Co 12:5-6 NIV).

At this point in his life, the great apostle went on the shelf for at least 10 years! Paul would spend three years in Arabia and a long period of time away. It would be over a decade before the church would send for him to begin the missionary journeys. What was going on during those ten years?

God was preparing Paul for something better! This man was to be the human author of half of the New Testament. He was to carry the gospel to the population centers of the western world.

Paul's conversion was a dramatic encounter of supernatural proportions. Blinded by the glory of God, he was knocked to the ground and heard the voice of Jesus. Three days later, his blindness was healed and he was filled with the Holy Spirit. One of the "goads" that led to Paul's conversion was no doubt seeing Stephen, the martyr, in communion with Jesus as he took his dying breaths. In those desperate final moments of his life, Stephen fled to the stairs and embraced the strength and peace of Jesus' presence! That day, Paul witnessed the reality of the spiritual world.

Paul learned the lesson of life and ministry on the stairs. A man of letters and learning, he had to lay aside even the power of his intellect in order to learn Christ.

> Now we have received, not the spirit of the world, but the Spirit who is from God, that we might know the things that have been freely given to us by God.
>
> These things we also speak, not in words which man's wisdom teaches but which the Holy Spirit teaches, comparing spiritual things with spiritual. But the natural man does not receive the things of the Spirit of God, for they are foolishness to him; nor can he know them, because they are spiritually discerned. But he who is spiritual judges all things, yet he himself is rightly judged by no one. For "who has known the mind of the LORD that he may instruct Him?" But we have the mind of Christ.
>
> 1 Corinthians 2:12-16

Paul had experienced an intimate relationship with Jesus in the Holy Spirit. Thereby, he had learned the things that one will never know in the natural. Paul spent over a decade alone with God so he could be a steward of God's mysteries.

> Let a man so consider us, as servants of Christ and stewards of the mysteries of God. Moreover it is required in stewards that one be found faithful.
>
> 1 Corinthians 4:1-2

Fifteen Lessons for Life

Paul could not talk in any detail about his intimate times with the Lord any more than we would talk about our intimacy with our mates! Yet,

Paul's letters resound with principles for living that sustain us to this very day! Heaven's power moves to earth when we meet Jesus on the stairs. Taking a walk through just one of Paul's letters, we find powerful declarations of what he learned on the stairs.

I have learned to be thankful for my spiritual family.

I thank my God every time I remember you. In all my prayers for all of you, I always pray with joy because of your partnership in the gospel from the first day until now, being confident of this, that he who began a good work in you will carry it on to completion until the day of Christ Jesus. It is right for me to feel this way about all of you, since I have you in my heart; for whether I am in chains or defending and confirming the gospel, all of you share in God's grace with me (Ph 1:3-7 NIV).

I have learned that prayer works!

And this is my prayer: that your love may abound more and more in knowledge and depth of insight, so that you may be able to discern what is best and may be pure and blameless until the day of Christ, filled with the fruit of righteousness that comes through Jesus Christ—to the glory and praise of God . . . for I know that through your prayers and the help given by the Spirit of Jesus Christ, what has happened to me will turn out for my deliverance (Ph 1:9-11,19 NIV).

I have learned that trouble can lead to victory.

Now I want you to know, brothers, that what has happened to me has really served to advance the gospel. As a result, it has become clear throughout the whole palace guard and to everyone else that I am in chains for Christ. Because of my chains, most of the brothers in the Lord have been encouraged to speak the word of God more courageously and fearlessly (Ph 1:12-14 NIV).

I have learned not to fear death.

I eagerly expect and hope that I will in no way be ashamed, but will have sufficient courage so that now as always Christ will be exalted in my body, whether by life or by death. For to me, to live is Christ and to die is gain (Ph 1:20-21 NIV).

I have learned that suffering is not always the result of sin.

For it has been granted to you on behalf of Christ not only to believe on him, but also to suffer for him" (Ph 1:29 NIV).

I have learned that I can think the thoughts of Jesus.

If you have any encouragement from being united with Christ, if any comfort from his love, if any fellowship with the Spirit, if any tenderness and compassion, then make my joy complete by being like-minded, having the same love, being one in spirit and purpose . . . Your attitude should be the same as that of Christ Jesus (Ph 2:1-2,5 NIV).

I have learned that God does the work in me.

It is God who works in you to will and to act according to his good purpose (Ph 2:13 NIV).

I have learned that to risk my life for Christ is worth it.

He almost died for the work of Christ, risking his life to make up for the help you could not give me (Ph 2:30 NIV).

I have learned that life at its best is knowing Christ personally and intimately.

But whatever was to my profit I now consider loss for the sake of Christ. What is more, I consider everything a loss compared to the surpassing greatness of knowing Christ Jesus my Lord, for whose sake I have lost all things. I consider them rubbish, that I may gain Christ and be found in him, not having a righteousness of my own that comes from the law, but that which is through faith in Christ— the righteousness that comes from God and is by faith. I want to know Christ and the power of his resurrection and the fellowship of sharing in his sufferings, becoming like him in his death (Ph 3:7-10 NIV).

I have learned not to quit!

Brothers, I do not consider myself yet to have taken hold of it. But one thing I do: Forgetting what is behind and straining toward what is ahead, I press on toward the goal to win the prize for which God has called me heavenward in Christ Jesus (Ph 3:13-14 NIV).

I have learned not to worry!

Do not be anxious about anything, but in everything, by prayer and petition, with thanksgiving, present your requests to God. And the peace of God, which transcends all understanding, will guard your hearts and your minds in Christ Jesus (Ph 4:6-7 NIV).

I have learned to think right.

Finally, brothers, whatever is true, whatever is noble, whatever is right, whatever is pure, whatever is lovely, whatever is admirable—if anything is excellent or praiseworthy—think about such things (Ph 4:8 NIV).

I have learned to be content.

I am not saying this because I am in need, for I have learned to be content whatever the circumstances. I know what it is to be in need, and I know what it is to have plenty. I have learned the secret of being content in any and every situation, whether well fed or hungry, whether living in plenty or in want (Ph 4:11-12 NIV).

I have learned I can do anything Jesus asks me to do.

I can do everything through him who gives me strength (Ph 4:13 NIV).

I have learned that God is my source of supply.

And my God will meet all your needs according to his glorious riches in Christ Jesus (Ph 4:19 NIV).

Paul learned all these fifteen great lessons of the abundant life as he sat at the feet of Jesus in the intimacy of the stairs. You too can have the revelation of life principles as you come to Him in that secret place.

Paul invented a word—*heavenlies* or "heavenly place"—when he reflected upon his supernatural experience. He wanted to express to us that there is a heaven we can go to now, while still on earth! We can be raised to "sit together with Him." It is a place of worship, authority, and warfare. The secret of a full life is found in our knowing we can have a "life abundant" now!

Remember, Paul wrote these thoughts down while imprisoned in jail in Rome. Your circumstances do not determine your attitude. You can worship and pray your way onto the stairs from anywhere! No matter the prison, the loneliness, or the turmoil that you face in your journey right now, be assured Jesus awaits you with loving arms in the secret place.

Chapter 15

The Bridal Chamber

Several years ago on a trip to the Middle East, I had the chance to go aside and stand on that little rock of an island called Patmos, the prison of the apostle John's exile. Sitting off the coast of Turkey, the island has very little to offer, just as in John's day. An old monastery, raised in the tenth century in honor of the great apostle, and a few old buildings dot the desolate land.

As I walked the rocky terrain, it was sobering to reflect upon John's commitment to Jesus. For his faith, John was arrested, torn from his beloved Ephesus where he served as pastor. Tradition relates that his captors tried to boil John in oil, but he refused to die. At last, they sent him away to this barren, forsaken bit of land, away from service, away from his congregation, and away from life as he knew it.

For most of us, this exile would have been the final blow. Where was God? Why would He let banishment be his pay after so many years of service? History indicates that John was past eighty years of age when his arrest occurred! This does not seem fair to our sense of logic. He was an old man—he should have been allowed to live out his days surrounded by all that was familiar, and be laid to rest among those he had held dear.

The truth is, God was about to do His greatest work in John! Yes, God had plans for even this senior saint! With no spectators except angels, John was to perform his greatest ministry. God was about to unfold the plan of the ages to him! John would see a panorama of the future. He would see the great climax of history, and the ultimate triumph of Jesus.

Let Satan torture you; let him exile you! Let the enemy drop you like a piece of garbage on a rock in the middle of the sea! But watch out—as long as you breathe, God still has an amazing plan for you! In the end, Satan will wish that he had killed you while he could have!

Worship on the Lord's Day

What do you do when you are thrown away? You simply worship! This was John's confession.

> I, John, both your brother and companion in the tribulation and kingdom and patience of Jesus Christ, was on the island that is called Patmos for the word of God and for the testimony of Jesus Christ. I was in the Spirit on the Lord's Day, and I heard behind me a loud voice, as of a trumpet.
>
> Revelation 1:9-10

In his isolation, John decided to start a worship service. There were no other participants, but His audience was Jesus, and that was enough! He was "in the spirit," for he was transported up those stairs and away to his Beloved.

In that place, he heard the Voice, and knew he was not alone. The Voice that had called him away from his Galilean nets and boats rang again in his ears. The Voice that had taught him amazing things stirred his soul. The Voice that had called his friend Lazarus from the grave now summoned John heavenward for an audience with God.

This is the voice of the One who had no beginning and no end. John was called to shake the church with the last words of Jesus before He comes back.

> "I am the Alpha and the Omega, the First and the Last," and, "What you see, write in a book and send it to the seven churches which are in Asia: to Ephesus, to Smyrna, to Pergamos, to Thyatira, to Sardis, to Philadelphia, and to Laodicea."
>
> Revelation 1:11

My friend, your suffering may be a summons to the stairs for destiny. Your problem is a pathway to a higher purpose. Quit your self-pity, for God is about to move you to destiny. Worship your way to a new beginning no matter what your circumstance.

A Look at Jesus

John turned to see the Voice. It had been nearly 60 years since Jesus had bid the disciples farewell and was lifted into heaven. But there in the secret place he'd found in the exile of Patmos, John saw Jesus again, standing in indescribable glory! One glimpse, and John fell out as a dead man! No man can stand in the light of God's glory!

It shouldn't surprise us that so many at our altars fall during ministry time. It is often too much to stand in the presence of God's glory and love. Prepare to fall before Him at your encounter! You may need to lie at His feet at the sound of His voice.

God gave John a clear view of the future. He saw the natural world and the spiritual world on a collision course with each other. He saw the church at her best and worst. He saw the judgment of every human system. He saw Jesus coming back for His own. He saw a new heaven and a new earth. God exploded the truth of the end of time right in front of John's eyes! Seals were opened, trumpets and bowls sounded forth and poured out their judgments upon the earth. The visions of the last war and, finally, paradise were revealed to John, who was an insider as he worshipped the Lord.

Sounds of Heaven

The book of Revelation contains much more than the sounds of war and the prophecies of end-time events. Here, we catch a glimpse of heaven. In the secret place of the stairs, John's two worlds mingled, and God allows us to hear the sounds of both.

The four living creatures, each having six wings, were full of eyes around and within. And they do not rest day or night, saying: "Holy, holy, holy, Lord God Almighty, Who was and is and is to come!" Whenever the living creatures give glory and honor and thanks to Him who sits on the throne, who lives forever and ever, the twenty-four elders fall down before Him who sits on the throne and worship Him who lives forever and ever, and cast their crowns before the throne, saying: "You are worthy, O Lord, To receive glory and honor and power; For You created all things, And by Your will they exist and were created."

Revelation 4:8-11

These heavenly scenes depict the joy that explodes from heaven on the day that the seven sealed mysteries are finally opened by the Lamb. In glorious and powerful images, the scarred Warrior, King Jesus, seizes the title deed to planet earth from the enemy, and declares the eternal deliverance of His creation from the clutches of the evil one. On the stairs, we learn the power of worshipping the worthy One!

Now when He had taken the scroll, the four living creatures and the twenty-four elders fell down before the Lamb, each having a harp, and golden bowls full of incense, which are the prayers of the saints. And they sang a new song, saying:

"You are worthy to take the scroll,
And to open its seals;
For You were slain,
And have redeemed us to God by Your blood
Out of every tribe and tongue and people and nation,
And have made us kings and priests to our God;
And we shall reign on the earth."

Then I looked, and I heard the voice of many angels around the throne, the living creatures, and the elders; and the number of them was ten thousand times ten thousand, and thousands of thousands, saying with a loud voice:

"Worthy is the Lamb who was slain
To receive power and riches and wisdom,
And strength and honor and glory and blessing!"

Revelation 5:8-12

Listen again to the celestial chorus, as the choirs of heaven join with the voices of the earth:

After these things I looked, and behold, a great multitude which no one could number, of all nations, tribes, peoples, and tongues, standing before the throne and before the Lamb, clothed with white robes, with palm branches in their hands, and crying out with a loud voice, saying, "Salvation belongs to our God who sits on the throne, and to the Lamb!" All the angels stood around the throne and the elders and the four living creatures, and fell on their faces before the throne and worshiped God, saying:

"Amen! Blessing and glory and wisdom,

Thanksgiving and honor and power and might,

Be to our God forever and ever. Amen."

Revelation 7:9-12

The Eternal Symphony

The music of the stairs stretches across all time! It was woven through Moses' song. It murmured gently in the still, small Voice heard by Elijah. It burst forth from the exuberant dances and high praise of David. It implanted itself deep in the desperate passion of Isaiah's hurting and hungry spirit. The music of the stairs is the Lamb's song! And Hallelujah, it is my song and your song in the middle of the mad pace of the twenty-first century. The symphony of the stairs is an eternal strain!

Then I saw another sign in heaven, great and marvelous: seven angels having the seven last plagues, for in them the wrath of God is complete. And I saw something like a sea of glass mingled with fire, and those who have the victory over the beast, over his image and over his mark and over the number of his name, standing on the sea of glass, having harps of God. They sing the song of Moses, the servant of God, and the song of the Lamb, saying:

"Great and marvelous are Your works,

Lord God Almighty!

Just and true are Your ways,

O King of the saints!

Who shall not fear You, O Lord, and glorify Your name?

For You alone are holy.
For all nations shall come and worship before You,
For Your judgments have been manifested."

Revelation 15:1-4

We can only echo the worship when we hear the swelling strains from the vaults of glory, "Worthy is the Lamb!"

Chapter 16

Become a Friend God Can Trust

It is a day that every father dreads, but also cherishes with all his heart.

My daughter Kelli was radiant as a bride! My heart swelled in pride and skipped a few beats as she met me at the top of the sweeping stairs. It was her choice to be married in the beautiful atrium of our church, with its winding stairways and open, glassed ceilings.

She descended gracefully down the staircase toward Kevin, her groom, waiting below. It made such a fitting picture as she neared the bottom of the steps, for she floated by the magnificent oil painting hanging there, depicting Jesus at the wedding in Cana of Galilee where He changed water into wine. Kelli had met the miracle of love and today was making it visible for all to see—a groom and a bride joined for earth's crowning relationship. I blinked back tears as Kevin met her on the stairs and escorted her into place for the ceremony.

At any wedding, I can't help but think of the greatest miracle: that our Heavenly Bridegroom longs to meet us on the stairs, to escort us into a deeper level of commitment and love for Him!

The Bride as a Unified Whole

Though I venture to the stairs of Jesus alone, I discover after a while that I am really not the only one there! The bride He has called away to a new springtime of love is a company, an army, a body.

In his letter to the Ephesians, Paul tied together the images of marriage and the union of the church to Christ. We hear Paul calling us as a bride to take our place at Jesus' feet. Our Lord longs to pour out His life and love upon us. He bathes us in the water of His Word. He transforms us into His very likeness. The call is stirring in this powerful passage:

> Wives, submit to your own husbands, as to the Lord. For the husband is head of the wife, as also Christ is head of the church; and He is the Savior of the body. Therefore, just as the church is subject to Christ, so let the wives be to their own husbands in everything.
>
> Husbands, love your wives, just as Christ also loved the church and gave Himself for her, that He might sanctify and cleanse her with the washing of water by the word, that He might present her to Himself a glorious church, not having spot or wrinkle or any such thing, but that she should be holy and without blemish.
>
> Ephesians 5:22-27

Brought Close to His Side

We are called not only to a newness of life, but to a glorious nearness in life. For too long, our salvation has been viewed as a contract instead of a communion. When we come to the Lord and receive His gift of salvation, we enter into a forever love relationship.

The longer I live, the more I am overwhelmed by Jesus' love for me. He wants me close, and He made the ultimate sacrifice to be sure I could be with Him. "But now in Christ Jesus you who once were far away have been brought near through the blood of Christ" (Ep 2:13 NIV).

The blood of Christ has given us access into His presence, and we find ourselves transformed and joined together with others who have experienced His transformation.

> But God, who is rich in mercy, because of His great love with which He loved us, even when we were dead in trespasses, made us alive together with Christ (by grace you have been saved), and raised us up together, and made us sit together in the heavenly places in Christ Jesus.
>
> Ephesians 2:4-6

No Longer In Bondage

As a part of the people of God, I have a new position. God saved me to raise me, not just at the rapture, but now! I am called to His throne! I am summoned to the secret of the stairs, the heavenly place, in Christ Jesus. My position is the same as my Lord and Bridegroom. I can be lifted above all my circumstances. No longer bound to earth, I soar above the junk that held me bound.

It is *together* we are saved. It is *together* we are exalted to sit with Jesus. This privileged spot at the feet of Jesus is for all of us to share, a joining experience.

God's Poems

Even now, God is writing a new biography of us all! "For we are His workmanship, created in Christ Jesus for good works, which God prepared beforehand that we should walk in them" (Ep 2:10). The word *workmanship* is the Greek word *poema* from which our English word *poem* arose. God is weaving our individual lives together into a heavenly lyric that will resound for His glory for all eternity. All the walls of separation must come down as we go into His presence.

> For He Himself is our peace, who has made both one, and has broken down the middle wall of separation, having abolished in His flesh the enmity, that is, the law of commandments contained in ordinances, so as to create in Himself one new man from the two, thus making peace, and that He might reconcile them both to God in one body through the cross, thereby putting to death the enmity. And He came and preached peace to you who were afar off and to those who were near. For through Him we both have access by one Spirit to the Father.
>
> Ephesians 2:14-18

By one spirit we have access to the stairs. God is enlarging the secret place. As we run up the stairs together, God is preparing a new place to live, and there is room for all!

Now, therefore, you are no longer strangers and foreigners, but fellow citizens with the saints and members of the household of God, having been built on the foundation of the apostles and prophets, Jesus Christ Himself being the chief cornerstone, in whom the whole building, being fitted together, grows into a holy temple in the Lord, in whom you also are being built together for a dwelling place of God in the Spirit.

Ephesians 2:19-22

We are not home, but we can visit that place of glory and unity in the realm of the Spirit. God's goal is to have one people with one purpose—to glorify the Lord Jesus Christ.

Driven to your Knees

The thought of this mighty movement of God, of making all people one in Christ, caused Paul to fall to his knees under the weight and hope of such a dream!

For this reason I bow my knees to the Father of our Lord Jesus Christ, from whom the whole family in heaven and earth is named, that He would grant you, according to the riches of His glory, to be strengthened with might through His Spirit in the inner man, that Christ may dwell in your hearts through faith; that you, being rooted and grounded in love, may be able to comprehend with all the saints what is the width and length and depth and height—to know the love of Christ which passes knowledge; that you may be filled with all the fullness of God.

Ephesians 3:14-19

Paul's prayer is for one great church—rich in glory, strong inwardly, to be indwelled by Christ, saturated by love, and filled with all the fullness of God.

"Impossible!" cries our carnal hearts, torn by our own issues.

"Never happen!" cries our religious division.

And yet, Paul saw the dream and believed it. God spoke the word and decreed it. We stand on the threshold today of seeing it happen—of fellow Christians laying aside petty differences and seeking the face of God together, finding the unity He gives in the Spirit, and being empowered to reach a world that is hurting.

This unity will happen, as Jesus becomes our goal. It will happen as one by one we hear the call of our Lord and love to "come away." The great secret of the stairs is the presence of Jesus Himself. Thousands of footsteps can be heard today of people running up those stairs into His arms. Will you go?

Now to Him who is able to do exceedingly abundantly above all that we ask or think, according to the power that works in us, to Him be glory in the church by Christ Jesus to all generations, forever and ever. Amen.

Ephesians 3:20-21

Secret of the Stairs

There is a place at the top of the stairs
Beyond my salvation
Beyond the door of prayer
There is a place
You're drawing me there
I'm waiting at the top of the stairs

There is a place where the battle's no more
Beyond the smoke that's rising
Beyond the wounds of war
There is a place
You're drawing me there
I'm longing for the secret of the stairs

Chorus
My love for you is no secret
You are the key
In You I find wisdom, revelation and peace
You've been waiting for me
I'm finally here
Open the door
I want to step in

There is a place
Where the river runs free
Beyond limits and shortage
Beyond human need
There is a place
Where the water is deep
I'm waiting will you take me there

There is a place where the Glory won't fade
Beyond a new anointing
Into the secret place
There is a place
You're drawing me there
I'm longing for the secret of the stairs

There is a place where I lose every care
Wrapped in your presence
A holy atmosphere
This is the place
I'm finally here
In your care at the top of the stairs.

Words and music by Angie McGregor

APPENDIX:

More Truths to Guide You Toward the Secret Place

Starting on the Stairs

Now therefore, listen to me, my children,
For blessed are those who keep my ways.
Hear instruction and be wise,
And do not disdain it.
Blessed is the man who listens to me,
Watching daily at my gates,
Waiting at the posts of my doors.
For whoever finds me finds life,
And obtains favor from the LORD;
But he who sins against me wrongs his own soul;
All those who hate me love death.

Proverbs 8:32-36

Your life can be better if you decide to make every day count. Nothing thwarts your God-given purpose quite like time wasted and opportunities missed, but opportunity is almost always just within your reach, resulting in fullness of life and a closeness with the Father as you've never experienced

In this great section of the Proverbs, Solomon, the wisest man who ever lived, wrote clearly that life is a "daily" event, revealing a simple pattern guaranteeing a life of favor. This pattern flows out of a renewed devotion to the Lord. We need a passionate longing for His presence to guide us daily. God's wisdom speaks, calling all of us to discover real life.

What steps can we take toward that discovery?

1. Learn to Listen and Stop Talking
"... Listen to me, my children ..." (Pr 8:32).

We must take time to hear our Lord's voice! God's voice is heard today in so many ways. God speaks to us from the pages of scripture. He also can speak to our spirits directly. Often He will speak through circumstances, through music, or through ministry. We can sometimes even hear His voice through the lives of others. Each day, we must learn to listen for that "still, small voice of God."

2. Keep Moving Toward God
"*. . . blessed are those who keep my ways*" (Pr 8:32).

If you have stepped away from God's direction, return to His purpose for your life! This may mean minor adjustments, or massive restructuring of your path, but the first step is the most important . . . make the choice to change!

3. Learn from Those Who Have Made the Climb
"*Hear instruction and be wise, and do not disdain it*" (Pr 8:33).

To continue on a path of experiencing real life, you should follow the words of wisdom given by leaders, mentors, and spiritual friends. Those you allow to speak into your life will affect your destiny. Get away from bad advice and embrace only wise counsel from those you trust.

4. Make Time Alone with God a Priority
"*Blessed is the man who listens to me, watching daily at my gates, waiting at the posts of my doors*" (Pr 8:34).

The time you set aside to wait before the Lord in meditation and intercession is time well spent! In this verse, notice the passion expressed, as the worshipper looks daily for the door into God's presence to swing open. In order to "watch" you must be awake—this pictures a person so in love with God that he will give up sleep to be in His presence. Daily discipline truly yields blessing!

5. Experience Life and Favor in His Presence!
"*For whoever finds me finds life, and obtains favor from the Lord*" (Pr 8:35).

As you operate in God's presence, wisdom, and strength, you can anticipate being touched and favored by the Father. The word "finds" here is a double affirmative in the Hebrew translation—it really means "finding to find." It is revelation knowledge! God's plan will appear and bring favor—a release of provision—even for those who do not know the Lord. Joy will permeate every area, need, and relationship.

You can decide now to start the climb! Nothing could be more rewarding to you than precious moments spent at the feet of Jesus. Blessing flows to the one who daily devotes time, attention, devotion, and passion to Christ.

Finding the Stairs During Disaster

For thus says the LORD: "After seventy years are completed at Babylon, I will visit you and perform My good word toward you, and cause you to return to this place. For I know the thoughts that I think toward you, says the LORD, thoughts of peace and not of evil, to give you a future and a hope. Then you will call upon Me and go and pray to Me, and I will listen to you. And you will seek Me and find Me, when you search for Me with all your heart. I will be found by you, says the LORD, and I will bring you back from your captivity; I will gather you from all the nations and from all the places where I have driven you, says the LORD, and I will bring you to the place from which I cause you to be carried away captive."

Jeremiah 29:10-14

Israel discovered life wasn't all rosy! They had lost their dream and had become a people captive to their enemy. In the middle of failure and disappointment, God speaks a word of hope: their dream from God was not destroyed, only delayed.

Perhaps life has thrown bitter disappointment into your soul. For some, this has been a season of catastrophe. Dealing with aftershocks of loss, failure, grief, and recovery can shake your faith and steal your dreams. Your God-given vision may have become distant and even impossible. The thing you always dreamed of may have evaporated before your eyes, and now you wonder whether your vision was ever meant to be. Hear this word of hope and take steps to rediscover your dream! God still has plans for you—comfort comes if you can get into His presence and listen.

Hold on to God's Promises
"I will visit you and perform my good word toward you . . ." (Je 29:10).

Disaster doesn't define you. Everything He has said about you and promised you is still true! God's word will be fulfilled. His delays are not His denials. God will correct His children, yes . . . but He will always keep His covenant with you!

Know God is Thinking Good Things About You!
"For I know the thoughts I think toward you,' says the Lord, 'thoughts of peace and not of evil . . ." (Je 29:11).

The God of this universe has you on His mind and heart! He longs for you to have the best in life. He knows where you are and will never leave you. On your worst day, when you feel like no one understands you, shares your dream, or has your best interests in mind, you can be assured that God is on your side! Sitting at His feet at the stairs, let His love flow over you and reassure your heart.

Embrace the Gift of Hope
". . . to give you a future and a hope" (Je 29:11).

Notice that God's gift is a future filled with hope! Literally this translates to mean "an expected end." The Hebrew words for hope refer to a rope tied to "what is at the end." No matter what storms we may face in life, our purpose is tied securely to God's eternal will!

Ask God for What You Need
". . . then you will call upon Me and go and pray to Me, and I will listen to you" (Je 29:12).

These words need no commentary! What an awesome promise to know God answers our prayers!

Seek God with All Your Heart
". . . you will seek Me and find Me, when you search for Me with all your heart" (Je 29:13).

In seeking God, you will find Him, know His heart, feel His presence, and in turn, find everything He has for you. The gospel writer recorded Jesus' words, "Seek first the kingdom of God, and His righteousness, and all these things will be added to you" (Ma 6:33).

As you act on the principles above, you will begin to rediscover your dream. Remember, God's thoughts and plans for you are bigger than your own, as Isaiah recorded: "'For My thoughts *are* not your thoughts, nor *are* your ways My ways,' says the LORD" (Is 55:8).

Can you see that the future is not dimly lit but is instead bright with the possibilities of God's favor and guidance as you walk with Him and seek His heart? Look ahead with confidence, for God delights in you!

Recommended Materials

Books and Devotionals

Bunyan, John. *Grace Abounding to the Chief of Sinners.*

Bunyan, John. *Pilgrim's Progress.*

Cape, David and Tommy Tenney. *God's Secret to Greatness.* Ventura, CA: Regal Books, 2000.

Chambers, Oswald. *My Utmost for His Highest.* James Reimann, ed. Discovery House Publishers (Barbour), 1992.

Franklin, Jentezen. *Fasting: the Private Discipline that Brings Public Reward.* Gainesville: Jentezen Franklin Publishing, 1984.

Lea, Larry. *The Highest Calling: Serving in the Royal Priesthood.* Lake Mary, Florida: Creation House, 1991.

Manning, Brennan. *Abba's Child.* Navigator Press, 2002.

Phillips, Ron M. *Awakened by the Spirit: Reclaiming the Forgotten Gift of God.* Nashville: Thomas Nelson, 1999.

Pickett, Fuchsia. *Stones of Remembrance.* Creation House, 1998.

Spurgeon, Charles H. *Morning and Evening: Daily Readings.*

Tenney, T.F. and Tommy Tenney. *Secret Sources of Power.* Shippensburg, Pennsylvania: Destiny Image/Fresh Bread Pub., 2000.

Tenney, Tommy. *The God Chasers—"My Soul Follows Hard After Thee."* Destiny Image, 1999.

Tenney, Tommy. *Up Where You Belong.* Nashville: Thomas Nelson, 2002.

Virkler, Mark and Patti. *Dialogue with God.* Gainesville: Bridge-Logos, 1986.

Music for Devotion

Angie McGregor, especially, *Most Holy Most High, Could We Dance?* and her 2005 release, *Water.* FacePlace Music, www.angiemcgregor.com.